What Others are Saying About This Book

"Newman's expert advice is clear and to-the-point. Speech software can dramatically boost your writing speed."
—Robert Cowart, author of *Mastering Windows 98* and *Windows NT Unleashed*

"I had used speech software for more than a year before finding this book. I wish I'd found it sooner! Any one of the tips on improving accuracy easily justifies the cover price."
—Harris Lilienfeld, M.D., Delaware Valley Pediatric Associates, P.A.

"After incurring RSI, I began using voice activated software as a necessity. With speech software and the expert advice of Dan Newman, I am not only able to work again, but I am even more efficient on the computer than before."
—Dede Leydorf, MPA, Member, Board of Directors,
     Independent Living Resource Center

"I wanted to save time with the latest speech recognition software, but I'm not a technical person. This book made it quick and simple for me to learn how to talk to my computer."
—Laura Raymond, Public Health Project Manager

"*Talk to Your Computer* saved me time and money. I learned what to buy, where to find it and how to get started with speech software. Highly recommended."
—Karl Arruda, Real Estate Attorney

"Working on a PC all day, I had fears of developing carpal tunnel syndrome. A friend recommended this book, and I have learned how to avoid carpal tunnel and get a lot more work done, all without endangering my health, or my career."
—Alisa Tanaka, Policy Analyst

Talk to Your Computer:

Speech Recognition Made Easy

by Dan Newman
Founder, Say I Can™ and say.i.can.com

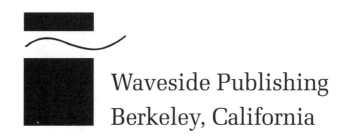

Waveside Publishing
Berkeley, California

Talk to Your Computer: Speech Recognition Made Easy
Dan Newman

Waveside Publishing
2039 Shattuck Ave. Ste. 500, Berkeley, CA 94704

Cover design: Pawlak Design. Author photo: Lisa Marie Hadley. Posture and products photos: Akeson Design. Posture illustration: Marilyn Hill. Layout: David Kamola, Get Set! Prepress, Oakland, CA. The author wishes to acknowledge the assistance of Sarah Murray in the research and drafting of materials for this book.

9 8 7 6 5 4 3 2 1

Printed on recycled paper.

Publisher's Cataloging-in-Publication

Newman, Dan, (Dan G.)
      Talk to your computer : speech recognition made
easy / Dan Newman. — 1st ed.
      p. cm.
      Includes index.
      LCCN: 99-90784
      ISBN: 0-9670389-3-6

      1. Automatic speech recognition. 2. Natural
language processing (Computer science) 3. Speech
processing systems—Purchasing. 4. Human-computer
interaction. 5. Consumer education. I. Title

TK7882.S65N49 2000   006.4'54
          QBI99-1082

Overview

Contents

Troubleshooting Poor Performance 141

Seeing the Future 157

Appendix: Further Information and Resources 175

Introduction

. . . .

"Computer!" That's how James T. Kirk and his successor, Captain Jean-Luc Picard, turn on the main computer of the Starship Enterprise. No bending over, no buttons to push, no typing at a keyboard. Seems nice, doesn't it—talking to your computer instead of typing?

Have you ever wished you could just tell your computer what to do? Talk a letter instead of type it? Print a page simply by saying, "Print page 3?"

Meet some people who do just that.

Scott Hagen, Vice-President, The Mechanics Bank

"I started using speech recognition for a simple reason. I hate to type," says Scott Hagen, vice-president of The Mechanics Bank in Walnut Creek, California. "I constantly use the computer in my job, but with the keyboard, I was never as fast as I'd like. I write credit evaluations all day. I've always felt that I would rather dictate than pound on the keyboard. After I'd completed the initial training, the program started working well for dictation almost immediately. It took me just a few days to get used to the commands."

Scott's hatred of typing is a common reason people get excited by speech recognition. His immediate success using speech software right out of the box is a little unusual—but with the tips you learn in this book, you too can achieve similar results.

George Morrison, Retired Construction Engineer

Retiree George Morrison is at the other end of the country and way of life from Scott. George lives on a 20-acre piece of land in Peterborough, New Hampshire that keeps him busy most of the time, with its one acre of lawn, flowers, an extensive vegetable garden, and many trees to trim. "I have plenty of everything except time," he chuckles. He started using the computer because he discovered that "your handwriting deteriorates exponentially with age." He discovered speech recognition later and now keeps up with friends and family writing letters and e-mail by voice.

George is a member of one of the fastest-growing groups of computer users in the country, senior citizens. He never had a chance to hate typing—he never learned to type in the first place. Now, with speech recognition software, he doesn't have to. He can write letters by just talking. He admits, though, that learning to use the software is not as simple as it first appeared and having a good book to help is essential.

Kristin Barendsen, Writer & Editor

Writer and editor Kristin Barendsen of Oakland, California didn't hate to type until she became stricken with repetitive strain injury (RSI) from overwork at the keyboard. She was on disability for a year. "I was a little bit afraid of going back to the computer. I was mad at computers at that point for having 'caused' my problem."

Kristin is a member of another fast-growing group of computer users—people who have become injured through overwork using keyboard and mouse. If speech recognition software had been around a few years earlier, she might not be injured now.

You'll meet some other users as you go along in the book. Their tips and cautions give a realistic sense of what it's like to use this software in daily life.

These people—just ordinary people using ordinary personal computers—have been able to talk to their computers and change their lives because of a new generation of speech recognition software programs designed for the mass market.

The first, Dragon NaturallySpeaking, was released by Dragon Systems in the summer of 1997. This program made computing history as the first software program to allow natural, rapid dictation to a PC. IBM quickly followed suit, introducing its ViaVoice series of dictation programs that helped drive the price of this software down to the realm of the affordable for the average American. Two other companies, Philips and Lernout & Hauspie (L&H), now offer continuous dictation speech recognition programs as well.

These amazing programs can transcribe your speech almost as fast as you can talk. Freed from typing, you can sit back, relax, and dictate letters, memos, and e-mail. It's an easy, natural way to write. This book, in fact, was written mostly by voice.

Why Buy This Book?

"Sounds great!" you say. "But I already know how to talk—why do I need a book about how to talk to my computer?"

For starters, speech recognition software will work only as well as your hardware and accessories permit. Besides a suitable computer, you need an appropriate microphone and, if you want to dictate away from your desk, a recorder. If you're serious about using speech recognition, you should be sure you have the best hardware for the job. Most computer salespeople don't have deep knowledge of speech recognition and how it works—even those who work for top name-brand manufacturers. This book gives you the information you need to configure your system well.

Then there's the challenge of figuring out what software program to buy. Speech recognition programs come in different shapes and flavors (and, of course, prices). Which program best suits your specific needs? Chapter 8, the *Buyers Guide*, describes the different products available and helps you determine what features really matter.

Once you have a computer and software program installed, you'll find that no speech recognition program is perfect. The program guesses what you said and often guesses wrong. There are many obstacles to reaching optimum accuracy, and overcoming these obstacles can be difficult without guidance. Chapters 4, *Tips for Achieving Top Performance*, helps you achieve the greatest possible dictation speed and ease with the least possible time and effort.

Talking to your computer might seem natural when you see it in a science fiction movie, but many people find actually doing it is strange and unfamiliar. You need to learn to deliver auditory rather than keyboard commands, as well as train the program to recognize your voice and vocabulary. You also need to develop skill in composing out loud. If you're used to composing on paper, or by typing, this will take practice. And figuring out the best ways to edit your writing by voice is not always obvious. Chapter 3, *Learning to Speak and Dictate*, provide tips and step-by-step instructions.

As founder of the speech recognition consulting firm **Say I Can**, I've had the pleasure of helping hundreds of clients use this technology successfully. I've tested dozens of systems and discovered what software, hardware and accessories achieve the best speed and accuracy. I've also helped hundreds of people just like you overcome their initial hurdles and frustrations by trouble-shooting all kinds of problems and coaching them to use the software most effectively. This book gives you the benefit of that experience in a distilled and accessible form, helping you choose the right system and achieve the best results, whichever program you choose to buy.

Who Should Buy This Book?

Almost anyone considering or currently using speech recognition software can benefit from this book.

If you're new to speech recognition technology, this book ensures you start off on the right foot by guiding you to the appropriate software, hardware and accessories. It also saves you months of trial-by-error learning (and frustration) by giving you instructions for teaching yourself to talk to your computer, solving common problems, and training your software to work as accurately as possible.

If you are already using speech recognition software but find that you are disappointed with its performance, this book gives you the tools you need to make the most of your existing investment. Despite what you might think, the problem is probably not your software. Using this book, you can find the optimal combination of hardware and accessories to work with your software. You'll also learn dozens of tips and tricks for interacting with your software in the best way and making full use of its tools to improve accuracy.

All users will benefit from the chapter on healthy computing, which draws on leading ergonomics experts to address ways of avoiding repetitive strain injury (RSI), one of the most serious chronic health problems that exists today.

Organization of This Book

This book contains four major parts. You may want to read the book straight through, or you may just want to use it as a reference, browsing through as you like.

Part 1: Talking to Your Computer—The Next Revolution

Part 1 introduces speech recognition technology in an understandable, accessible way.

Chapter 1, *Why Talk to Your Computer?*, describes the different types of speech recognition programs and who can benefit from them.

Chapter 2, *Is Speech Recognition Right for You?* explains what you need, in terms of both hardware and expectations, to make speech recognition software practical.

Part 2: Learning to Talk to Your Computer

Part 2 tells you what you need to know to work most effectively with your software.

Chapter 3, *Learning to Speak and Dictate*, gives you a host of practical suggestions for getting used to talking to your machine and writing out loud.

Chapter 4, *Tips for Achieving Top Performance*, delivers just what its title promises, distilling the experience of dozens of users into one pithy chapter. If you have been using speech recognition but have been dissatisfied with its performance, you should zip right to this chapter.

Chapter 5, *Keeping Healthy While Computing*, delivers some important information about how to maintain your vocal health when using speech recognition software on a regular basis. It also delivers the most current recommendations from ergonomics experts about how to set up your workstation to lessen the likelihood of experiencing repetitive strain injury (RSI), which is becoming epidemic among people who use computers heavily.

Chapter 6, *Structuring Your Workflow*, suggests the most practical ways to use speech recognition software in an office where you need to coordinate workflow with others. It offers guidelines for working with assistants who may be correcting work you have dictated into your computer or a recorder.

Part 3: Setting Up for Speech Recognition

Part 3 gives you the technical information and guidance you need to buy the right system and get it running smoothly.

It begins with Chapter 7, *Understanding How It Works*, which explains how the computer translates your words from sounds to printed page. Understanding the basics of the technology can help you make the right choices in hardware and software as well as make you better understand why the programs work (or don't work!) the way they do.

Chapter 8, the *Buyers Guide*, gives you a selective guide to everything you need to set yourself up for speech recognition. It describes key features of software, microphones, and recorders, selectively listing only the best and most useful tools.

Chapter 9, *Troubleshooting Common Problems*, gives advice about fixing the most common computer problems encountered when using speech recognition software.

Part 4: Looking Ahead

Chapter 10, *Seeing the Future*, takes off on a flight of fancy, exploring the future of speech recognition in the home and in society. As amazing as this technology is right now, it is still in its infancy. You'll get some glimpses into the future as I speculate about where speech recognition may lead us.

The Appendix, *Further Information and Resources,* describes a variety of Web sites, news groups, and other useful sources of information for using speech recognition. It also lists manufacturers who offer innovative products that make use of speech recognition technology.

Conventions Used For Easier Reading

This book uses a few special conventions to direct your attention.

Tips give you useful shortcuts and additional information.

Alarms signal you to take care so you don't lose work, risk injury, or suffer other unhappy accidents.

Cross-references refer you to other locations in the book for further information.

Why Talk to Your Computer?

I know a young woman I'll call Ann, a student at a prestigious East Coast university. Ann is bright, engaging, and a hard worker. She's enthusiastic about school, immersing herself in her classes and in the vibrant campus life.

Ann has only one problem—but it's a big problem when you're a student at a top university: Ann has dyslexia and writing papers is like sweating bullets and just as bloody.

At least, it *was* that difficult until she discovered that she could talk to her computer instead of type. She now composes her papers by voice and has one of her roommates proofread the final product before she hands it in. Her dyslexia no longer stands in the way of her self-expression on the page.

I know a man named Bruce, who you will hear more from later in this chapter. Bruce is long past college and is busy with a full-time securities law practice. His work is heavily research-based and also involves a great deal of writing. He estimates he spends ninety percent of his workday using the computer.

Bruce had a problem too—he belongs to a law firm in Los Angeles but he prefers to live in San Francisco.

At least, it *might* have been a problem a few years ago. Today, Bruce uses e-mail and dictation software that enables him to do all his own document review and brief preparation. He can work out of his home half the time and travel to the L.A. office only when necessary. His speech recognition software, he says, is like his own private secretary, available twenty-four hours a day.

Why should you talk to your computer? The answer is simple: You can work in new ways and make new things possible. Using the latest speech recognition programs, you can write more rapidly, increase your productivity, and free yourself from being chained to your computer, chair and keyboard—even your office!

Over the past twenty-five years, we've all become used to using our computers in a particular way, as an input device controlled by mouse and keyboard. This chapter explains the different types of programs available and offers you some reasons why you might be motivated to change your ways and your relationship with your computer.

If It's So Great, Why Isn't Everyone Doing It?

"At the tone, please speak your account number into the phone. When you're done, press the pound sign." Have you ever been through this routine on the telephone? Then you have used speech recognition before.

In fact, almost everyone is talking to computers without knowing it. Limited vocabulary speech recognition programs have been used for years by telecommunications companies, credit card companies and a few other big businesses to cut down on customer service costs and improve response times. You're not talking to the box that sits on your desktop, of course, but to the large corporate computers that these companies now use to keep records and bill customers.

However, it's still very new for computers to be able to understand and transcribe natural, continuous human speech like the kind I used when dictating this book. As noted in the introduction, it was only in the summer of 1997 that the first such program was introduced on the consumer market.

Before 1997, there were a number of speech recognition programs available for consumers. However, they were based on an older technology and required you to speak in a stilted, unnatural voice and pause between words. They were anything but natural. Their accuracy was also poor. Many people eager to try talking to their computers tried these programs and were disappointed because they fell so far short of the marketing hype. Although the new generation of software is vastly improved, many people became skeptical of any claims on behalf of speech recognition programs and are reluctant to try them again.

Bruce MacLeod, Securities Lawyer

Bruce's tone of voice is what you might expect for a securities lawyer: measured, dry, quiet, precise. You hear his voice, and you expect a man who thinks carefully before he speaks.
He says of his own introduction to speech recognition software, "I'd experimented before with IBM and the earlier version of Dragon, which were basically not very usable programs. I'd played with them but never really used them efficiently or effectively. They just weren't good enough."

Many people have purchased and installed current versions of the programs but have become frustrated because using the software isn't as easy as they thought it would be. They didn't realize that, as good as the programs are, they still aren't going to write those letters or reports for you. Just like fancy new drawing programs won't make you an artist, dictation software won't suddenly make you a writer. They also didn't realize that it would take some work to make the program work really smoothly and well.

Bruce MacLeod, Securities Lawyer

Bruce didn't let himself be discouraged by his early experiences. When Dragon NaturallySpeaking was released in 1997, he was one of the first to buy and install it.
What was his experience? He says in the same even tone, daring disbelief, "It's fabulous. The best piece of software ever

written... It was pretty much usable right out of the box after I did the training routine."

When asked to offer advice for people considering buying speech recognition programs, his voice becomes animated. "Just do it! I can't understand why everyone doesn't do it."

Bruce admits, though, that "you have to understand how the program works, how it thinks, how the correction routine works, in order to make it work most effectively. And that isn't really obvious to most users. Most users don't give enough thought to how they train it... The program is pretty good out of the box but it's only really as good as you train it to be."

What Is Speech Recognition?

So what are we talking about when we say "speech recognition?"

Speech recognition is an umbrella term that covers a number of different approaches to creating software that enable computers to recognize natural human speech. Though related in concept to computers that speak to you, technology that lets you speak to your computer works quite differently.

On the big business level, *limited vocabulary* speech recognition systems enable you to talk your credit card number into the phone instead of punching buttons, or respond to simple questions from an automated voice mail system.

On the consumer level, there are two broad tasks that speech recognition programs enable you to accomplish: dictating text to your computer, and controlling your computer by speaking commands instead of typing them. These two types of tasks are referred to as *dictation* and *command and control*. While a few programs focus exclusively on command and control, most enable you to carry out both tasks.

Command and Control

Command and control features enable you to control a computer or machine through your voice instead of typing commands from the keyboard or clicking a menu item with your mouse.

Command and control applications were the first consumer application to be developed successfully because they use a limited vocabulary that users speak in discrete blocks. They don't require any understanding of grammar, word usage or spelling—the banes of any writer's existence! They have long been used by people with physical disabilities that prevent them from using the keyboard.

Command and control applications are similar to the limited vocabulary speech recognition systems in terms of the underlying technology. While these original programs required users to speak in a rather artificial, stilted voice (as described earlier in this chapter), newer programs with command and control features accept natural speech.

At the moment, most of the command and control features available for the home user assume the graphical interface with command bars and menu as their basic environment. Instead of moving your mouse, you speak to your computer, telling it to open menus and choose commands.

Nowadays, most available speech recognition programs offer a combination of command and control and dictation features. However, a few programs, like voice Web browsers, focus on command and control exclusively, with very limited dictation abilities.

For information on the different programs with command and control features that are available, see the "Software" section of the Buyer's Guide, page 116.

Dictation

Dictation features enable you to talk to your computer and turn your talk into text. The dictation program "fools" the computer into thinking you're actually typing. You can then edit, print, and save that text like any other computer document. Most dictation programs also enable you to command and control your computer too.

The four most popular commercial speech recognition software programs—Dragon NaturallySpeaking, IBM's ViaVoice, L&H Voice Xpress, and Philips FreeSpeech—are dictation programs. They are impressive—what could be more exciting than watching your words appear on the computer screen as you talk? They make the dream of a Star Trek future seem real. They are also the programs that give you the most immediate and dramatic improvement in productivity.

Learning to write by talking to your computer is harder than just telling it commands, though. That's why this book focuses on using speech recognition to perform dictation.

Dictation programs don't really understand you. If you started to tell a dictation program about your problems with your boss or the pain in your tooth, it wouldn't react any differently than if you read it part numbers from a ball bearing catalog. They also require that you train them to understand your specific voice and vocabulary. The initial training period, called *enrollment*, involves you reading on-screen text to the computer.

The enrollment process typically takes about 30 minutes, although training time continues to drop with each new program version the manufacturers release. Correcting the program and teaching it your special speech patterns and vocabulary takes a period of interactive work, typically about 2-3 weeks. You don't have to put in this much work, but as with anything in life, you get out what you put in. The more time you invest training your program, the more accurate it will become in transcribing your voice.

There are two different types of dictation programs: Discrete dictation and continuous speech recognition. I discuss each type further below.

For details on programs with continuous dictation features, see the "Software" section of the Buyer's Guide, page 116.

Discrete Dictation

Discrete dictation programs represent an older technology that developed before computer hardware or software could easily process naturally spoken, continuous speech. Discrete dictation programs require the user to—speak—like—this—that is, with clear pauses between words, to help the program separate one word from the next. Discrete dictation makes it easier for the computer to understand you but harder for you to talk to your computer.

Discrete dictation programs soured many people on speech recognition because it requires an unnatural way of speaking that most people don't like. (That's why Dragon named their new generation program "Dragon NaturallySpeaking." It spoke to what people wanted that they hadn't yet found.)

However, discrete dictation programs are still on the market because they can be the best choice for:

▶ People who have absolutely no hand use.
▶ People with heavy accents or distorted voices.
▶ Programmers.

Continuous Speech Recognition

Continuous speech recognition has been the Holy Grail of speech recognition technology. With continuous speech recognition, you can talk to your computer at natural speeds without any special pauses or emphases and have it understand and transcribe your speech. In short, you can write with your voice. This is closest to what you've seen in the movies—and it's possible today with the leading commercial dictation programs.

It's Fine for Someone Else, But Why Should I Do It?

Doctors, attorneys and others who compose text daily have long known that dictation is a fast, efficient way to write. Writing by voice lets you get your thoughts on paper quickly —faster even than expert typists. In fact, if you're a professional already accustomed to dictation, you'll find the transition to using speech recognition quite easy.

Don Goldmacher uses speech recognition to dictate medical reports.

Don Goldmacher, Psychiatrist

Psychiatrist Don Goldmacher, like most physicians, was already well acquainted with talking into a machine. For many years, he dictated lengthy reports and other professional writing into a recorder and paid a typist to transcribe the tapes. Curious about speech recognition, he decided to give it a try. He found it easy to make the switch. However, he wasn't sure if using speech recognition would really pay off. The results? He had to try it for a while to see.

You no longer have to be a well-paid professional with a typist to work by voice. With the emergence of programs like ViaVoice and Dragon NaturallySpeaking, anyone with a PC can work the way only a fortunate few could before. Used well and with the proper equipment, the software acts as your own personal secretary, with 24-hour availability and virtually instant transcription. These programs can type what you say at 150 words per minute—if indeed you can speak that quickly!

Learning to compose out loud is an investment in your lifetime productivity. The sooner you start working by voice, the sooner you'll reap the benefits of improved speed and ease. Even though the technology will inevitably change, the basic skills you learn now will serve you long into the future.

Bruce MacLeod, Securities Lawyer

Bruce MacLeod has found that using dictation software has "vastly improved my productivity. I draft briefs three times faster now. But where my dictation software really shines is in document review. I can work in a different way now, really, because I can read documents and find portions that are interesting. I then just dictate the interesting portions directly into my database, and there I have it, captured, coded, and ready to use.

"It's pretty inefficient for a lawyer to type large sections of a document into a computer. Lawyers have to read the documents anyway; it takes only seconds to read in the full paragraph, and then I can just plug it into a database, and I'm done. That's by far the greatest speed enhancement. I don't have to edit or think in-between. I work in a totally different way.

"I use a database designed for lawyers that isn't made any more. I dictate into my dictation program's word pad and then I cut and paste. I've found that's the most efficient way of working."

Speech Recognition, Workplace Injuries, and Physical Disabilities

Another good reason to consider speech recognition software is that, physically speaking, we weren't really designed to use keyboards—not to mention sit at desks all day! Many people find using a keyboard difficult. Some people type slowly or never learn to type at all. Some have hand injuries or other disabilities that make typing or sitting for prolonged periods of time difficult or impossible. Speech recognition is the keyboard alternative. If you can't type or just don't want to—or have back problems that require you to stand or vary your posture frequently—you can talk to your computer instead. With this software, you can do almost anything by voice that you could do with keyboard or mouse.

Repetitive Strain Injuries Are Epidemic

That we weren't made to use keyboards has become painfully evident as more and more people are becoming injured through heavy keyboard and mouse use. Typing and clicking can cause or exacerbate damage to muscles, tendons and nerves. Sitting in a static posture for hours with arms raised and fingers flying puts an unnatural load on the muscles of the upper back and arms. Almost everyone feels discomfort and stiffness while typing, and an alarming number of people are developing a painful condition called repetitive strain injury (RSI).

While most people think carpal tunnel syndrome when they hear the term RSI, repetitive strain injuries (also known as cumulative trauma disorders, or CTDs) can involve many other parts of your hands, arms, wrists, and upper body. They all involve strain and overuse of the delicate tissue of tendons and small muscles. Once damaged, these tissues are hard to heal. Cautions Deidre Rogers, a registered nurse and ergonomics expert, "Most people who become injured in this way go many years before they can resume hand-intensive activities."

Carpal tunnel syndrome accounts for only about 5% of RSIs. Other common problems include Thorassic Outlet Syndrome, which is like carpal tunnel syndrome of the upper back, and tendonitis of the thumb, hands, elbows and shoulders.

The problem is epidemic. Since 1981, the incidence of repetitive injuries has increased more than 20 fold, from about 15 per 1000 to more than 320 per thousand in 1994 to become the largest category of reported worker illness and injury. According to the U.S. Department of Labor Bureau of Labor Statistics (BLS), repetitive injuries resulted in the longest median absences from work—17 days—of any frequent type of work-related injury and cost the country billions of dollars in health care and lost productivity.

The BLS estimated that 332,000 Americans suffered from RSI in 1994. However, experts agree that these BLS statistics underreport the incidence of RSI because the BLS does not survey self-employed workers or federal, state, and local employees. Also, many employees fail to report problems with RSI to their employer but try to "work through the pain" for fear of being fired. Taking these factors into account, the American Public Health Association estimates that more than 775,000 workers suffered from RSI in 1995. A group of Harvard physicians estimated the number of people suffering from RSI in 1998 to be as high as 2.8 million.

A repetitive strain injury forced Kristin Barendsen to start using speech recognition.

Kristin Barendsen, Writer & Editor

The number of people who suffer RSI may be great, but RSI happens just one person at a time. It happens to people like Oakland-based writer and editor Kristin Barendsen. "I had a repetitive strain injury caused by typing. I was temping as a word processor and typing six hours a day. I quickly got bad enough in my arms and shoulders so it really hurt to type or use a mouse. I stopped using the computer altogether, hoping my condition would improve." It didn't, and Kristin began investigating other possibilities. The price of computers was just beginning to drop (it was 1993) and she decided speech recognition was worth a try.

While people who use computers at work are not the only type of worker afflicted with RSI, the BLS acknowledges that "the rapid growth of computer-based jobs involving intensive keying has increased the incidence of RSI problems."

Overcoming RSI with Speech Recognition

Many people with severe RSI become partially disabled, unable to use their arms normally and certainly unable to type or use the mouse. While therapy and exercises can help many people with RSI recover basic functioning, going back to the keyboard and mouse brings back the same old problems. Speech recognition software can help people with RSI remain productive and employed. Perhaps more importantly, it can help prevent these injuries in the first place. Depending on your state's labor regulations, your employer may even be obligated to provide you with appropriate technology, including voice recognition software, to help address physical problems you experience that are precursors or signs of RSI.

Kristin Barendsen, Writer & Editor

So how did speech recognition software work out for Kristin? "My dictation software has allowed me to go back to work. I work close to full-time these days, including at least three hours a day on the computer. I wouldn't attempt to have the career that I have without speech recognition software."

Her RSI hasn't gone away, though—it's something she lives with still. "RSI isn't something that seems to go away totally for most people. I still feel it when I type, although I can do most other things pretty well."

Kristin has her frustrations with the speech recognition program she uses, but she says firmly, "I would recommend speech recognition software to anyone, even people with healthy arms, as it might help prevent RSI."

I also know about RSI from personal experience. I first learned to use speech recognition software after I became injured from overwork at the keyboard. Speech recognition software was pretty primitive then, but even so, it was a far better alternative than abandoning my graduate studies. Learning to use speech recognition software enabled me to finish my degree and to continue to be productive in my work life. My business manager, Chris, also came to speech recognition through the unfortunate route of severe RSI and now does all his work by voice.

Even if you've never felt a twinge from the keyboard, speech is still a more comfortable way to work. You can sit, stand, move and even stretch while dictating. Why wait to become injured before changing your habits? Take advantage of this amazing technology now and save your hands for better things.

Is Speech Recognition Right For You?

When you see someone else use speech recognition, it looks like magic. As any magician will tell you, though, magic is more than meets the eye. It takes time, practice and patience to perfect magic tricks—including setting up a speech recognition system that really works well.

This chapter aims to give you realistic expectations and a good understanding of both the possibilities and limitations of the current technology. In my experience, people almost always find it's worth the investment in the end, but I've also seen people become frustrated and give up because they expected everything to be easy and without work on their part. Taking a few minutes to read this chapter now will save you oodles of frustration later. You may even decide that speech recognition technology is not right for you, at least not yet.

Start with Realistic Expectations

User George Morrison's reaction to first seeing speech recognition software used is typical. "I thought it was really neat!" he says.

Like George, most people are excited by the idea of talking to their computers because it seems so easy and natural—after all, that's how we communicate with each other every day, and it seems we do it without effort. Many people, when they hear about speech recognition, think, "Great! I hate computers, and now I won't have to learn to use them at all. My computer will do as I command!"

Well, think again. Only in Hollywood does technology work flawlessly and without human effort. You yourself took years to be able to recognize human speech, let alone make others understand you! Mastering typing takes time and practice too. While speech recognition is an amazing technology that will ultimately make your life and work much easier, you need to train the program to recognize your voice and your vocabulary. You must also adapt your work habits to make the most effective and error-free use of the technology.

Don't Expect a Miracle

We all have expectations conditioned by years of watching TV and movies where the impossible is done in the blink of an eye. Don't let go of your sense of wonder over speech recognition, but don't expect a miracle either. Speech recognition programs aren't perfect. They make mistakes in transcribing what you say, and you have to take time to go back and correct these text errors. You may also experience the same kinds of problems you do running any other kind of computer program, like occasional crashes and conflicts with other devices and programs on your system.

You Still Must Learn Computing Basics

Just as with any computer program, you need to master some computing basics before you can use speech recognition effectively. If you've been using computers for a while, you probably have the skills you need already. If you're new to computers, you'll find you can use speech recognition more effectively if spend a little time learning about these computer basics:

▶ Organizing and managing your files (for example, saving, opening, and closing files, creating new folders or directories, and navigating on your computer).

▶ Understanding the basics of the Windows operating system, including choosing menu commands and opening and closing programs.

▶ Attaching accessories to your computer through the various ports in the back of your computer.

You Need to Speak Clearly

In ordinary conversation, most of us mumble and slur words together. When talking to other people we can mumble and still be understood because people have an incredible ability to pull meaningful patterns out of very limited information. Computers, you'll be glad to know, are nowhere near as smart or adaptable as we are. To achieve accurate results, you need to speak clearly to your computer or it will have difficulty recognizing your words.

Many people aren't aware when they are mumbling. You may find it useful to use your program's ability to replay your dictation to listen to yourself talking to your computer.

A good trick is to pretend you're Dan Rather or Katie Couric reading the news, or imagine you're delivering a speech to a small group. You may end up speaking more loudly than in normal conversation but that's fine.

You Need to Have Patience

Computers may move in nanoseconds but they deliver results in ordinary human time. You need to have patience when setting up your speech recognition system because it takes time for the computer to learn your speech patterns and vocabulary. You also need to enter proper names and other special vocabulary words into the program and correct the program's mistakes. Don't think of your computer as a super-sophisticated, brilliant machine—think of it as a rather slow three-year old child who you're teaching to understand you.

George Morrison, Retired Construction Engineer

What advice does George give new users? "Read your manual and refer to it frequently. I keep reading it but I can't remember it all, so I have to read it again! And you have got to be very patient and keep trying. That's it!"

Consider the Tasks You Want to Accomplish

You can use speech to do anything that you can do by keyboard and mouse. Some tasks, however, are easier than others. The software works best for dictating letters, memos and other text, and for commanding and controlling your software programs to perform basic tasks.

Speech is more cumbersome to use for editing text you've already created. Editing existing text requires mixing commands and dictation, and the computer will sometimes confuse the two. For example, you might say "bold last line" and the computer will type "coldest lime." If this happens often, frustration kicks in and you'll find yourself reaching for the keyboard and mouse.

Speaking clearly and having patience can reduce or eliminate this type of error, and editing by voice can be quick, useful and effective under the right conditions. However, editing does require additional practice and patience compared to the ease and speed of rapidly dictating first drafts to get your thoughts on paper.

Like text editing, using spreadsheet and database programs by voice mixes dictation and commands. It likewise requires more learning and practice than dictating straight text.

Peter Trier, Philosopher, Writer, & Disabled Rights Activist

If you're disabled and considering speech recognition, Peter Trier advises that you "talk to three or more people you know who use the equipment, preferably people who have the same disability as you do." If you don't know of any others who fit the bill, seek out Internet forums for speech recognition users and/or people with disabilities and post a message posing your questions.

Evaluate Your Own Characteristics

Be realistic about your own skill level and mental habits before putting speech recognition into practice. You can then choose software and hardware that is appropriate for your specific needs.

Can You Type?

Though speech recognition software unchains you from the keyboard, speech recognition programs like NaturallySpeaking, ViaVoice, Voice Xpress and Philips FreeSpeech still require correction and input of new vocabulary words. Typing with the keyboard is still the most effective way of entering this information, as typing is precise where speaking is ambiguous. If you do not know how to type but are physically able to, are you willing to learn at least to hunt and peck? If not, you'll find that teaching the program new words is more difficult, and you may not achieve top accuracy.

George Morrison, Retired Construction Engineer

George Morrison came of age in a time when he didn't need to use computers or type to do his job. "I never learned to type," he says, "I still type with two fingers." He tries to correct by voice but often finds it slow, inaccurate and frustrating and resorts to the keyboard instead.

Do You Have an Injury or Physical Disability?

If you have an injury or disability that prevents you from using the keyboard or limits the amount of time you can spend sitting at your computer, you probably have a strong motivation to make speech recognition work for you. Strong motivation makes your chances of success high. Your disability might affect the speed at which you can get your program to achieve maximum accuracy, though. If you're not able to type or sit at the computer for long periods, you won't be able to correct the computer's mistakes as quickly. If you have problems with your voice or speech articulation, the program will take longer to recognize your words correctly. However, the payoff is great—you can write, communicate with others and work at the computer without depending on your hands.

If you don't have any use of your hands (or feet) at all, you will likely have better success with DragonDictate, an older form of Dragon NaturallySpeaking. This program, a discrete speech recognition program, requires you to speak with pauses between words but requires less correction and can be used much more effectively without a keyboard.

How Familiar Are You with Computers?

Are you a total "newbie," as they say on the Internet—new to computers without a lick of experience? Or are you already an old salt of the computer high seas? Or somewhere in-between?

Speech recognition is a pretty complex process that involves the coordination of microphones, a sound card, and your speakers and software, among other parts of your computer. This book has a troubleshooting section that suggest solutions to common, general problems, but no book can anticipate every problem or know the specifics of your computer. While you don't need to be a computer expert, you are more likely to be satisfied using speech recognition software if you are already familiar with computers or have a friend, family member, or trusted local vendor who can help you if you encounter problems.

George Morrison, Retired Construction Engineer

George Morrison retired in 1981, before computers were common equipment in executive suites. That's why he never had to learn to type. He says, "I had to read computer-generated reports, but actually to handle a computer, well, I hadn't touched one until my wife gave me one seven years ago for our 50th anniversary. I wasn't sure I needed a computer, but my wife couldn't think of anything else I needed, I guess, so she got me one! I'm glad she did, although she hears me cussing at the thing once in a while."

George Morrison began using a computer when his wife gave him one for their 50th

George didn't start using speech recognition right away. His friend Tom, who he met through CompuServe, introduced him to it, "and I thought it was pretty neat." He's now on his third computer, one he bought especially to use with speech recognition because he found his previous computer was too slow.

He admits that learning to use the program well requires more work than he thought at first. However, he says, "I've never felt intimidated by the thing. I've been pretty much self trained. If I have a major problem, I just call up Tom and he straightens me out."

How Do You Learn New Software?

If you understand how you best learn a new computer program, you'll be able to go about learning speech recognition software more effectively. Do you learn best from a book? By trying things out yourself? By learning from someone else? Are you willing to just fool around with a program to learn its commands and possibilities, or are you afraid your computer might blow up if you take a wrong turn somewhere?

say.can.com

If you learn well by experimenting and testing things out yourself, you're a natural for teaching yourself speech recognition software. If you learn well from books, check out Say I Can's manuals. These "how-to" guides help you learn to use specific software programs as quickly as possible and are written in the same easy style as this book. (Sample chapters are available online at SayICan.com.) If you learn best from others, investigate locally available training or consulting services. Many community colleges and adult education programs now offer reasonably priced computer courses at convenient times.

What Is Your Budget?

Speech recognition software demands a lot of system resources. Your system will work best if you can afford high quality software, hardware and accessories. While you can get speech recognition to work on less expensive systems or systems that don't have the ideal combination of components, typically they work more slowly and deliver less accuracy and you may not be satisfied with the results.

I drafted this book on a Pentium 233 MHz machine. Like most people, I don't like to buy a new computer unless I really need one. I'm finding the newest version of the program often runs too slowly for me, though, and I have a feeling I'll soon be upgrading to one of those blazingly fast 450 or 500 MHz machines. Since I do a lot of writing in my work, I know I won't be satisfied unless I have faster performance.

The bottom line: consider your current budget realistically in relation to the quality you need and expect.

If you just want to write letters to family and friends and browse the Web in combination with also using the keyboard, you may do fine with a less expensive system.

If you have more demanding uses in mind, like preparing documents for your business where time and accuracy are of the essence, or using speech recognition software because you have a physical disability that prevents you from using a keyboard, you may not be satisfied with a less expensive system and will want to invest in better hardware and high-end software.

Investigate Alternate Funding Sources if You're Disabled

If you have a physical disability, you should investigate alternate sources of funding for your computer system. Under the Americans with Disabilities Act, government-funded agencies are required to take all reasonable efforts to ensure that people with disabilities have equal access to services. Depending on your situation, your insurance company, local school system, or other governmental agencies may help pay for your system. Church groups and local branches of Computer Professionals for Social Responsibility may also have funds or be able to refer you to other groups that do.

Where Does Hardware Quality Matter Most?

Because the key components of a speech recognition system—software, RAM, processor, microphone, and sound card—all work together, deferring purchase of some components until you have more money doesn't work as well as it might with some other computer applications. However, if you find yourself in that position, it's best to get the best software and sound card that you can up front. Or, if you're a Windows 98 user and have a USB (Universal Serial Bus) port on your computer, consider a high-quality USB microphone. USB microphones don't need a sound card, as they use circuitry built-in to the microphone to process your voice signal before sending it to the computer. You'll still want a sound card for your computer so you can play sounds and music, but you won't need to worry about getting the best and most expensive. With either of these two choices—good sound card or USB microphone—the speech files you create when initially training your software program will be of the highest quality and you'll get the most out of RAM and processor upgrades.

Meet Some Systems

The users who are profiled in this book have computer systems that range from models that would now be considered outdated to a souped up, superfast Pentium 500MHz that doesn't even hesitate when transcribing your words. Their accuracy varies too, and while accuracy isn't always related to system specifications, it's clear that the system does matter. The systems used by Kristin, Don, and Scott are representative of most of the profiled users.

Kristin Barendsen uses Dragon NaturallySpeaking on a Pentium 166 with 96 MB RAM and a 1.2 gigabyte hard drive. When she bought her system about three years ago, the Pentium 166 was the fastest processor available. Now, though, she observes, "As Dragon gets better and demands a faster processor speed, I can see that my system is becoming outdated. The other day, I caught up on my filing as it typed a paragraph!" She reports that her accuracy is "average." Kristin does the most varied writing of all our profiled users, a key factor affecting accuracy.

Psychiatrist Don Goldmacher, who routinely dictates lengthy examination reports of twenty pages or more, achieves accuracy of 95 to 98 percent. His computer has 128 MB of RAM, a Sound-Blaster 64 sound card and an AMD K6-400 Processor, a mid-range processor in terms of speed. He benefits from using the Dragon NaturallySpeaking Medical edition, which includes specialized vocabulary suitable for his work.

Scott Hagen, vice president of The Mechanics Bank, uses a Pentium III 500 with 128 MB of RAM and a Turtle Beach sound card. He's been using Dragon NaturallySpeaking Professional edition for four months and had excellent results right out of the box. He writes routine letters and memos and dictates credit evaluations directly into the computer.

Frequently Asked Questions

Since speech recognition programs are still pretty new, most people have questions about how they work and what they can really do. This section answers the questions I most commonly hear in my daily work with users investigating speech recognition.

How Well Does It Work?

Most people achieve speeds of 100 to 140 words per minute, not including time spent correcting mistakes. Accuracy after initial enrollment and a few weeks of training ranges, for most people, from 90 to 98 percent. In practical use, accuracy is more important than speed, since mistakes are time-consuming to correct. The users profiled throughout this book report accuracy results ranging from a low of 80 percent to a high of 98 percent.

The three most important factors in how well speech recognition works are what I call the "three S's"—your **s**ystem, how you **s**peak, and **s**ticking to it.

Your System

Your software, sound card, microphone, processor speed and RAM all affect how well speech recognition works in practical life. For recommendations, see "Do I Need a Supercomputer?" below.

How You Speak

Dictation software can type what you say about as fast as you can speak, as long as you speak clearly. Some people, like profiled user Don Winiecki, naturally speak in a slower, clear voice. "I guess I'm lucky," he said, "because the program has an easy time picking up my voice." You can be successful with speech recognition even if you aren't a naturally slow speaker, though; the key is to articulate your words. My business manager, Chris, writes entirely by voice since he has a severe case of RSI. His speech is naturally rapid, but he gets good recognition results because he has learned how to talk to his computer.

The type of writing you do also affects accuracy. If most of your documents are relatively similar to each other in vocabulary and tone, your computer will probably make fewer mistakes than if you typically dictate on a wide range of topics. If you dictate on a range of topics, the computer has less past context information to guess what you said, so it tends to makes more transcription errors.

Sticking to It

How well your system performs also depends on your dedication in sticking with the program. You need to continue to use the program over a period of a few months and put some effort into correcting its mistakes in order for the program to perform well. As you correct the computer's mistakes over time, the software learns your voice better and is more accurate. Practice also allows you to get used to the speech software's verbal commands and to adapt to writing by voice if you're used to composing by keyboard.

Do I Need a Supercomputer?

No, you don't need a supercomputer. Almost any new computer you buy will be acceptable for using with speech recognition software. For best performance, choose a computer with 128 MB of RAM. More RAM is fine too, although it won't necessarily improve performance of your speech recognition software. Buy the fastest processor that meets your budget—at least 400 MHz—and a good sound card. As faster processors are developed, new versions of the speech recognition programs are designed to take advantage of the new fast processors. In general, you will always be best off to buy the fastest computer you can afford.

Understanding Hardware Basics

The processor (or CPU) is the traffic cop of your computer. It processes all instructions and commands—which include not only the commands you select but a lot of behind-the-scenes commands. The higher the number of megahertz (MHz), the faster your processor and the faster your computer—if you have enough RAM and a fast enough data bus to handle the fast processor speed.

RAM stands for Random Access Memory and it's the short-term memory of your computer. Commands and other information move between the processor and other parts of your computer through RAM. Generally speaking, the higher the number of your RAM, the more programs you can use at the same time and the better your computer's performance. (At a certain point, though, your software may not be able to take advantage of more RAM.) The performance of speech recognition software depends partly on how many vocabulary words the computer can "remember" at one time—which depends on your computer's amount of RAM.

Minimum System for Acceptable Performance

The minimum system requirements for using speech recognition programs vary depending on the software, and they're printed on the box and in the user manual. Always read these requirements carefully. Below are listed the minimum system requirements for using the most common speech recognition programs now available:

▶ Pentium (or equivalent) 233-MHz processor.
▶ 64 MB of RAM.
▶ Sound card.
▶ Microphone.

You typically need at least 200 MB of free hard disk space as well. Some of this space is required to install and store the program files. You also need to have a certain amount of free hard drive space to run the program. Just as you can't work effectively on your desk if every available space is piled with file folders, your computer can't easily move files between RAM and permanent storage if you don't have a certain amount of free hard disk space.

If you're running a Windows system and want to find out how much free hard disk space you currently have:
1. Double-click the My Computer icon on your desktop.
2. Click the disk you want to check.
3. Open the File menu and click Properties.
You'll see a pie chart that shows how much used and free space you have on your disk.

Minimum requirements, however, are just that. To use the software productively you'll need more memory and processor speed than the minimum. You can easily install more RAM yourself to add to what you have or buy a new microphone. Upgrading your processor or sound card requires a little more time and money. Unless you're handy with computers, you'll want to have a computer technician do the work.

Best System for Superior Performance

You'll be much happier with your speech recognition system if you buy a system that has all the power under the hood you need. You'll also be better set to use the next generation of speech recognition software, which is being designed with the assumption that users will have machines with processor speeds of 400-550 MHz.

Based on four years of experience configuring speech recognition systems for hundreds of users, I recommend the following system configuration:

- ▶ The fastest processor available (currently, 500 MHz).
- ▶ 128 MB or more of RAM.
- ▶ A sound card with very clear signal.
- ▶ A high-quality microphone designed especially for use with speech recognition.

For more information on microphones, see the section "Microphones" in the Buyers Guide, page 125.

Sound Card Recommendations

A sound card is a circuit board that allows the computer to play sound through speakers and to receive sound through a microphone. Before the advent of speech recognition software, users only cared whether the computer could play sound. Sound card makers focused on improving playback quality for music and games.

Speech recognition uses the other half of the sound card—the listening half. As you speak, your voice generates electrical impulses in the microphone. The sound card converts these impulses into numbers that your speech recognition software can analyze. Good sound cards faithfully measure the electrical changes your voice generates. Bad sound cards introduce static and interference, making it difficult or impossible for your program to accurately determine what you said.

Avoid Integrated Sound Cards

Most sound cards work fine for speech recognition. However, I strongly recommend you avoid "integrated" sound systems. In these systems, the sound circuitry is built in as part of the motherboard, the main computer circuit board that holds the processor. Many computer makers use this type of sound system. While this saves money for computer manufacturers, the sound wiring is physically closer to other circuitry and thus more likely to allow electric interference to degrade the quality of the speech signal. For best results, ask your vendor to install a separate, non-integrated card.

If the system you buy has an integrated sound card and it gives poor results, you can still install a regular (non-integrated) card and disable the integrated one.

USB Microphones: The New Alternative to Sound Cards

Another option if you run Windows 98 is to buy a USB (Universal Serial Bus) microphone, which plugs into a USB port in the back of your computer. USB microphones process the sound signal directly in the mic and don't route your voice through the sound card, so the quality depends only on the mic. Only a few USB mics are available now, as the technology is relatively new. However, USB is becoming the new standard for connecting equipment to the computer so a wider range of USB mics should be available soon.

Sound Cards that Deliver Good Results

Users report excellent results with two popular sound cards, the SoundBlaster 64 AWE and the Turtle Beach MultiSound Fiji Pro series. Many other cards also work well. Dragon Systems regularly tests sound cards and posts the results on their Web site, www.dragonsystems.com. You should be able to get one of these cards included with your computer no matter where you purchase it. Like extra memory (RAM), the card you want will probably not be included in advertised computer packages. You need to ask to add these options to your system. Any computer vendor will be happy to oblige. If you're adding a sound card to a system that has integrated sound, ask the computer vendor to disable the integrated sound circuitry when assembling your system.

Can I Use It With My Operating System?

Most speech recognition software to date has been designed and created for Windows operating systems. You can use all the programs listed in the Buyers Guide with Windows 95 and Windows 98. You can't use them with earlier versions of Windows or on DOS-only systems (although with most programs you can command DOS from within Windows 95 or Windows 98).

You can use most but not all of these programs with Windows NT. Your ability to say commands (like menu commands) is limited in Windows NT.

If you're a Mac user, no continuous dictation software currently exists. At the time this book was written, however, IBM had demonstrated a prototype of ViaVoice for Macintosh. In addition, Dragon Systems announced plans to develop a Mac product based on Dragon NaturallySpeaking. A small company called MacSpeech has a command and control program called ListenDo (originally called MacDoIt) available. Check out their Web site for the latest information on their products.

If you're a Linux user you're in luck, as IBM has made a big push to make its successful ViaVoice program available on Linux. ViaVoice is included in Red Hat's most recent version of Linux, and IBM says it intends to offer ViaVoice through other Linux distributors, including Caldera, the other major commercial distributor of Linux software.

IBM is hosting a Web site for new Linux-related speech recognition technologies and program downloads. Visit www.software.ibm.com/speech to find information about the Linux site; follow the *Linux* option in the long list of Web links.

What Program Should I Buy?

You need to consider what your primary use of the software will be. Each program has its own strengths and weaknesses. Which is best for you depends on the types of tasks you want to carry out and the applications you use most frequently.

You also need to consider your available hardware. Some editions of each program demand more RAM, hard drive space and/or processor speed than others.

The four general purpose, large vocabulary dictation programs are:

- ▶ Dragon NaturallySpeaking (made by Dragon Systems).
- ▶ FreeSpeech (made by Phillips).
- ▶ L&H Voice Xpress (made by Lernout & Hauspie).
- ▶ ViaVoice (made by IBM).

For introductory information on these and other speech recognition software products, see the "Software" section of the Buyers Guide, page 116.

Each of these companies offers a number of different editions of their main program.

Speech recognition software is a very competitive and rapidly changing area right now. New products and new versions of existing products appear every week as the big four try to outdo each other, so the best program for a specific task today may no longer be the best program tomorrow.

Is It Expensive?

say ı can .com

Expensive is a relative term. Only you can decide what's expensive for your budget. However, home editions of speech recognition software are no more expensive than computer games or other basic computer programs. You can also find speech recognition programs bundled together with other programs in a cost-saving package. For example, Corel bundles a limited edition of Dragon Naturally Speaking with their WordPerfect office suite, and IBM bundles ViaVoice with the Lotus office suite. You can buy the basic editions of each of these programs independently for about $60. Prices fluctuate, of course—you can find the current pricing on most products on our SayICan.com Internet site.

Don't be hasty to buy on price alone. Inexpensive basic editions tend to lack important features. Buying a lower-end product will lead quickly to frustration if the product won't dictate into the applications you need, includes an inferior microphone or has other important limitations.

If you're aiming for the best results—as most people using speech recognition are—you'll be much happier buying the more expensive and full-featured editions. Prices for the higher-quality consumer programs are around $150 from all four manufacturers. If you're looking to buy speech recognition for use at your office or in another professional setting, or you're just looking for the highest quality you can find, the prices range from $150 up to about $600, depending on the software you choose and any specialty vocabularies you might need.

Keep in mind that you may need to buy a microphone as well. While all the programs include a microphone in the package, many users find that purchasing a higher-quality microphone separately improves both comfort and performance. If you plan to use the software regularly, budget $100-200 for a good quality mic that you feel comfortable using daily.

Is It Hard to Learn?

There are two parts to learning a speech recognition program. First, the computer needs to learn your particular voice. When you first start using the program, you read to your computer for about twenty minutes so it can learn your voice. After this initial training, the program works at about 85-90 percent accuracy, which will gradually improve over time as you use the program more and correct its mistakes.

The second part of learning the program is learning to use the specific program features and commands. Out of the box, dictation programs are great for just talking and having your words appear onscreen. However, learning to correct by voice, navigate your computer by voice, or create automated commands like, say, adding a letterhead with a single command, takes some learning and practice, just as with any other computer program.

Can I Dictate into Any Programs I Want?

You can dictate into pretty much any Windows 95 or Windows 98 program. (I haven't encountered any programs it *doesn't* work with, although there may be some.) Attorney Bruce MacLeod, who you met earlier in this chapter, dictates extensively into Microsoft Excel with excellent results. Many of the profiled users, including Kristen Barendsen and Don Winiecki, dictate into Microsoft Word. Some lower-cost editions of speech software let you dictate only to a few specific programs, so be sure to verify that the edition you buy will dictate into the applications you commonly use.

If you're considering buying a program or other product that has a speech recognition program included with it, be sure to check carefully whether the included edition is the same as the full-featured edition sold independently. Many of these so-called "bundled" editions of speech recognition programs have a limited set of features and do not allow you to dictate into other programs.

How Long Until I Become Productive?

How quickly you can become productive depends partly on your needs and definition of "productive." You can become productive at a lower rate of accuracy very quickly. After just twenty minutes or so of reading into your computer to train it to recognize your voice, you can begin dictating letters, memos, and reports at about 90 percent accuracy. You'll still need to correct the program's mistakes (or have someone else correct them) and format your document.

If by "productive" you mean working in the most efficient and accurate way possible, it typically takes two to three months for users to learn the program well, create macros and other shortcuts (if your edition enables you to do so), and input specialized vocabulary words such that your program works at peak efficiency.

Can I Fire My Assistant?

Don't fire your assistant just yet. Text that you write using speech recognition also still needs to be edited, formatted correctly, printed, and processed, just like text you create any other way. Speech recognition programs also make mistakes and someone needs to correct them. You can delegate this task to your assistant if you wish. However, your assistant's productivity will improve enormously as the computer takes over the bulk of the transcription work. So start thinking of ways to better use his or her skills!

Don Goldmacher, Psychiatrist

Don Goldmacher used to routinely dictate long reports and summaries of medical records into a tape recorder and pay a typist to transcribe the tapes. He now dictates into a Sony digital Minidisc recorder and has Dragon NaturallySpeaking Medical do the initial transcription. His typist? She now acts as a proofreader, listening to Don's recorded speech on the disc and correcting the transcript. "The software has cut my transcription costs by two-thirds!" Don enthuses. Just as important, when he needs a rapid turnaround but his typist is not available, he can now get immediate results by dictating directly into his computer.

3

Learning to Speak and Dictate

I'll be honest. Speech recognition marketing hype suggests that you can talk to your computer just like you talk to a friend. The truth is—you can talk to your computer in all kinds of ways your friends would never tolerate!

When you're trying to impress someone at a cocktail party, you'll probably try to speak in complete, grammatical sentences. If you lose your train of thought in the middle of a phrase, your new acquaintance might look at you strangely.

Talking to the computer is different. The computer doesn't care about your grammar or word choice, or even if you're silent for minutes at a time. It doesn't care if you're in a bad mood or unfriendly. It does notice, however, if you slur your words together or mumble. And while you can speak to your computer in natural tones and at natural speeds, you need to learn its special lingo for executing commands.

Most of us have had limited experience conversing with our little gray boxes—besides cursing at them when they crash. To speak effectively into your computer, you'll need to unlearn old habits and gain new skills. This chapter tells you how.

Want to hear some samples of people speaking to their computers? The IBM speech recognition research unit has audio samples on their Web site of people speaking in commands, discrete dictation style and continuous dictation style. Jump to: www.research .ibm.com/hlt/html/desktop_recognition.htm

How to Talk to Your Computer

Your first step in learning to use speech recognition software effectively is learning to speak in a way that helps the computer record your words accurately.

Speak Clearly

In conversation, people tend to mumble and slur words together, knowing others will still understand what they say. If you say "Jeet?" your friend will understand it as "Did you eat?" Computers, however, are less adaptable than people. To achieve accurate results, you must speak clearly. Pretend you're Dan Rather or Katie Couric reading the news, or imagine that you're giving a presentation to a small group. You may end up speaking louder than usual, and that's fine. For a useful exercise, see "Moving Your Mouth," below.

Moving Your Mouth

Read aloud a sentence from this book. Make a point of slurring your words and mumbling. Then read the sentence again, clearly. Can you tell what you're doing differently in these two readings?

Make a big smile. Notice what it feels like to raise the corners of your mouth. Next, pucker up your lips and push them out, as if you're making an exaggerated kiss. Notice the muscles

around your mouth that make your lips move. Then, drag the corners of your mouth into a frown.

Try reading the same sentence three more times—once smiling, once puckered-up, and once frowning.

Did you notice a difference in sound quality? Pitch? Clarity?

Now let your jaw relax. Gently massage your jaw muscles, your temples, the sides and front of your chin, the muscles beneath your eyes, and the area above your upper lip.

Finally, sit up straight at your computer and read the same sentence again. The idea is not to speak louder, or to "push" words out. Just read calmly and clearly. How does this feel different from mumbling?

Voice exercises like those singers use can also be useful. It may help to imagine that talking is giving the corners of your mouth a workout. Don't exaggerate your sounds or force them. Speak normally, just more clearly.

Pronounce Each Word

When we listen to someone speak, our ears receive an unbroken stream of sound. Our brains automatically separate this sound into words. We reconstruct words that are only partially heard—or left out altogether. Here's an example.

Read this sentence out loud to a friend, standing so that she cannot see your face. Notice that the sentence is missing a word—to be grammatical, it should say "to a computer."

"The book I'm reading is about speaking to computer."

Have your friend repeat back what she heard. Chances are, she'll fill in the word "a" to make the sentence grammatical.

Because our brains reconstruct missing sounds so easily (especially small, common words like "a," "the," and "of"), in everyday speech we tend not to pronounce every sound and word. It's just not necessary.

A computer transcribing speech tries to reconstruct missing sounds, too, taking its best guess at what you actually said. However, the computer isn't as smart as a person and often guesses wrong. For accurate transcription, it's important to make sure every word you say to the computer is pronounced, not "missing." A sentence that is perfectly understandable to a person might not be clear enough to a computer.

This change in speaking style does not mean that you have to slow your natural pace. The leading programs allow you to speak up to 150 words per minute—which is probably faster than you normally talk. Just be sure to speak clearly and pronounce each word.

Pause If You Like

Your friends might think it odd if, during an animated conversation, you halt mid-sentence to gather your thoughts. When speaking to the computer, though, you can pause as long as you like to think, take a break or arrange your notes. Your computer won't get bored waiting for you.

Give It Context

Your accuracy will increase if you speak in complete sentences, because the computer has more context to use in deciphering your sounds. Speaking one word at a time usually decreases accuracy. So concentrate, think of the right words, and speak them as a continuous stream.

Leave Out Fillers

Speech recognition programs will usually mistake "uh" and "um" for "a," "of" and similar-sounding words. Unfortunately, since "uh" and "um" sound so much like these words, there is no way to make your computer ignore them. To learn to stop saying "um," practice being silent instead of saying something to fill the space. When you feel an "um" coming on, just say nothing. Saying "um" can be as addictive as nail biting. Still excising these filler words from your speech has an added benefit. Besides achieving greater accuracy in dictating, you'll also sound more polished, articulate and confident.

Speak with Inflection

When talking to the computer, people tend to imitate the robotic voices of computers in old sci-fi movies. But generally speaking, using a flat monotone will reduce your accuracy as well as put you to sleep. Keep photos of friends next to the computer and pretend you're speaking to them. This will help you use more natural tones and will brighten your day too.

Breathe Fully

Breathing fully and sitting straight will help you speak clearly. (It also helps keep your voice healthy.) If you slouch while dictating, your lungs will be compressed and your voice constrained, making it harder for the computer to understand your words. The breathing exercise below can help you notice what it's like to breathe more fully.

Breathing

While seated, put your hand lightly on your belly. Breathe in and out slowly from the top of your chest, without letting your hand move. This is breathing "shallowly." Now breathe in so that your belly expands, moving the hand that's resting on it. When you breathe out, your belly (and hand upon it) should move back to its original place. This deeper breathing can help you speak more clearly and may make you feel healthier in general.

Close Your Eyes

Dictating while looking at the screen tends to be distracting—it makes your speech more hesitant and less natural. Try dictating with your eyes closed. Most people get significantly better results this way. If your boss thinks you're taking a nap, try looking at the wall or at the photos of your friends—or a chart showing your increased productivity since you starting talking instead of typing!

Be Alert

When it's 4:00 a.m. and you're still dictating the proposal that's due tomorrow, your computer knows that you're tired. Tired people tend to mumble and speak without energy, which makes your accuracy decline and means you'll have to spend more time doing manual corrections. You'll get your best results when you're most alert—and this will save time in the long run.

Relax

Stress and tension change voice quality and degrade recognition accuracy. When you're new to speech recognition software, you might be a bit anxious as you speak, anticipating that the computer will make mistakes (or that it won't like you!). The computer does make mistakes, of course, and frustration may kick in as you see the mistakes proliferate. Frustration makes you more tense, changing your voice, which generates more mistakes, more frustration and still more mistakes.

Stress and tension can contribute to injuring your voice too. For tips on keeping your voice in shape, see "Maintaining Good Vocal Health" in Chapter 5, Keeping Healthy While Computing.

Errors are inherent in computer transcription (as in human transcription). The computer takes its best guess at what you say, and it often guesses wrong. Correcting mistakes is part of the normal process of using speech recognition. When you learned to type, correcting errors became second nature. With the right attitude, correcting speech recognition errors can be just as routine.

Learn to Laugh

It helps to have a sense of humor about the computer's errors, and the computer is great at generating real howlers of mistakes. Speech recognition software tries to fit what you say into something that makes grammatical sense, if not literal sense. So its weird guesses often fit right into your sentence. You say "fresh squeezed lemonade" and the computer types it right out: "fresh grease lemon aid." Don't try *that* beverage at home!

For more blooper examples, see "Real Life Bloopers" in Chapter 7, Understanding How It Works. Got your own examples? Visit the Say I Can Web site and share your laughter!

say.can.com

Working at the computer is not especially good for your body. We were not made to sit in place for hours at a time, arms forward, fingers twitching rapidly. The repetitive motions of typing can cause discomfort and, in some cases, serious injury. It doesn't help that the intensity of computer work can lead people to neglect their bodies, posture and physical positioning for hours at a time. Many computer users have an association, conscious or unconscious, between using the computer and being tense.

For information on staying healthy while talking to your computer, see Chapter 5, Keeping Healthy While Computing.

Muscle tension can make your voice tense, changing its pitch and quality. Recognition programs tend not to respond as well to tense voices. Achieving high accuracy takes some unlearning of the common "computers = tension" equation.

Working towards better results with speech recognition software can actually help you develop healthy habits. Good posture, rest, exercise and meditation not only improve general well-being but also, amazingly, make your program recognize your voice better. At last, computer use that encourages health!

Learning to Dictate

Like any skill, dictating to your computer takes practice to do well. I wrote my high school papers by hand, before the personal computer age, and in college, after computers had become widespread, I continued to write papers longhand, typing them into the computer from my notes. Gradually I became more adept at typing and started composing by typing into a computer directly.

Years later, a repetitive strain injury caused by too much computer use forced me to give up keyboards. With much writing to do and unable to afford a secretary, I turned to speech recognition software as a keyboard replacement. At first, composing out loud—never mind speaking to the computer—felt strange and unnatural. The mechanics of watching the computer screen, correcting mistakes, and editing text by voice constantly interrupted my thought process. I dealt with this by handwriting first, then dictating the handwritten words into my computer.

Writing by voice engages a different thought process than typing or writing longhand. Like the transition from handwriting to typing, it took effort and practice for me to master this change. But after years of practice, I now write almost everything by voice—including this book! For myself and for hundreds of thousands of other speech software users, dictation now comes naturally—as much or more so than the unnatural, but learned, skills of typing and handwriting. The lesson is that what seems natural is just a function of practice and time.

How to Compose Out Loud

Besides learning how to speak with articulation and in the right tones, you also need to learn to compose aloud, which is a distinct skill of its own. Even experienced writers, who are already used to thinking in complete sentences and paragraphs and imagining how words will look on a page, can't compose out loud right away.

Start by Reading

We all learned to type by copying printed passages. The best way to learn to dictate is to begin the same way—by copying. By dictating something already on paper, you can practice learning the voice software without having to worry about composing sentences at the same time.

Choose a letter, memo or e-mail message typical of your normal writing. Then read it into the computer as if you're speaking to another person. You'll need to say your punctuation aloud—for example, "comma," "period," and "new paragraph." Look away from the computer, focusing on the page. As you read, pretend the computer isn't even there. (It won't be offended!)

Donald Winiecki, Professor

Don uses a digital recorder and frequently tapes conversations he has with a graduate student assistant for later transcription. I was surprised at this, since today's speech recognition software isn't usually very successful at transcribing conversations. One reason is that you must say punctuation aloud. Don confesses, though, that "I speak the punctuation, and she frequently speaks the punctuation as well."

Don has become so habituated to speaking in his software's style that "sometimes I'll make a mistake when I'm talking to someone and slip in some punctuation!" His friends and family get a good laugh out of it—but Don gets the last laugh, since he's the one who saves time and trouble using speech recognition to get his thoughts down on paper.

Don Winiecki dictates into a portable digital recorder that his computer then transcribes.

Reading aloud will help you get used to talking to the computer. After a bit of practice, add in a few sentences of your own thoughts. By starting to compose out loud interspersed with reading, you'll overcome any natural inhibitions you might have.

Fear of Dictating

If you feel inhibited or self-critical when talking to the computer, remember that the computer doesn't care what you say or how you say it. It's easiest to start writing by voice when no one is around, and you should ensure this privacy when learning. Practice will make you less self-conscious. If your computer makes mistakes while you're practicing, just laugh at them and fix them later.

Be Easy and Chatty

When learning to compose by voice, start with what's easy. Try dictating a few sentences about today's weather, make a list of things to do, or compose a chatty letter to a friend.

It's easier to dictate when you're not looking at the screen. Look at the ceiling or close your eyes. This will help you avoid distraction, relax and let your thoughts flow.

Build Up to Complex Writing

Save more difficult documents for later, after you're comfortable composing simpler texts by voice. In the meantime, continue to prepare complex writing in your usual way, such as by typing. To dictate on complex topics, you'll need the skills of both speaking properly to the computer and composing intricate prose by dictation. It's best to practice these skills one at a time.

Only after you're skilled at more casual, "chatty" compositions should you dictate documents that:

▶ Have difficult or complex subject matter.
▶ Follow a detailed outline.
▶ Use complex sentence structure.
▶ Are aimed at a demanding audience, such as professional colleagues.
▶ Will be widely circulated.

Dictation Tips

This section offers you a grab bag of tips to help you make the most of dictating to your speech recognition program.

Be Complete

Speak in complete sentences, or at least complete phrases. Think of what you're going to say before you say it. Composing a sentence in your head before saying it will help you maintain your train of thought.

Your High School English Teacher Was Right

For complex writing, outlining is key. For, say, a detailed letter, write or dictate a few words summarizing the main point and subpoints of each paragraph. When you're dictating, look at the outline. You'll naturally expand the outline to complete sentences as you speak.

Let the Train Roll On

When you're writing a first draft, capture your ideas as fast as you can get them on the screen. Don't try to edit as you go—you can come back and edit later. Tell yourself to keep talking.

Focus on the Gain

If you need extra motivation to get over dictation hesitancy, think of all you have to gain from writing out loud. Imagine boosting your output by double. Imagine filling the screen with text without having to type. Relax your hands, arms and shoulders and think how nice it is not to have to bang away at the keyboard.

Imagine Your Audience

As in any writing, keep your audience in mind. Imagine the particular person you're writing for to help the dictation flow.

Find Your Natural Style

Composing aloud, your writing style may change. Some people find that their spoken style is less polished and more conversational. I find it easy and rapid to dictate first drafts, then go back and revise later. Typing for me is laborious and interrupts my thought process, though my typed writing requires less editing afterwards. You might be pleased with your new, spoken style, teach yourself how to compose aloud in your "old" style, or use a combination of dictating and revising to get the results you want. Use whatever method you prefer.

Become the Writer You Were Always Meant to Be

Using speech recognition can be a good way to get over writer's block. Imagine you're telling a friend what's next, then tell the computer.

Henry James Dictated Too

Author Henry James wrote his novels longhand—until 1896. Pain in his right wrist, probably from writer's cramp, the 19th century version of RSI, lead him to hire a stenographer so that he could write out loud. The switch to dictation changed his style. Wrote a biographer, "the spoken voice was to be heard henceforth in James's prose, not only in the rhythm and ultimate perfection of his verbal music, but in his use of colloquialisms, and in a greater indulgence in metaphor." Friends claimed they could pinpoint the exact chapter in What Maisie Knew *when handwriting ended and dictation began. (From* Henry James: A Life *by Leon Edel)*

Plan: Learning to Dictate

Finding it hard to get started? Here are some suggestions:

1. Read to the computer to get used to talking to it. Review the tips on how to speak to your computer to get the best possible accuracy while reading.
2. Compose simple sentences about the weather, then move on to notes to friends.
3. Outline a letter or memo several paragraphs long. Dictate the letter from start to finish based on the outline.
4. Continue outlining and dictating. If you like, experiment with making a mental outline instead of a written one. Some users eventually compose entirely in their heads, while other continue to make outlines, even if they write only a word or two for each outline point.

4

Tips for Achieving Top Performance

Imagine a speech recognition system that performs perfectly—making no mistakes and typing your words instantaneously. A utopian vision? Maybe. But you can take concrete steps toward improving your computer's accuracy.

A 90 percent accuracy rate translates into about twenty-five mistakes per page, while a 95 percent accuracy rate is around thirteen mistakes per page. This five percent difference in accuracy means you spend half as much time correcting—and much less time feeling frustrated! A small improvement in accuracy can be the difference between speech software being a productive, useful tool versus it being too frustrating to use.

The level of accuracy you can expect depends on many variables, including:

▶ How much time you spend training your computer.
▶ The speed of your computer.

▶ Your sound hardware.

▶ The quality and placement of your microphone.

▶ The type of text you dictate.

▶ How clearly you speak.

▶ The noise level of the room in which you're dictating.

After you complete your program's initial training, the program should type at least 80 percent of your dictation accurately. As you use the program over several weeks and correct its mistakes, the software will learn your voice better and its accuracy will improve. Most people can achieve an accuracy rate between 90 and 98 percent.

Peter Trier, Philosopher, Writer, & Disabled Rights Activist

Peter Trier has his own perspective on accuracy. Peter has a progressive genetic disorder called Spinal Muscular Atrophy that leaves him largely bedridden. He's been using DragonDictate since 1993. (Like many people with disabilities, Peter finds that his distinctive breathing and voice patterns make continuous speech software too inaccurate and unreliable for his needs.) He depends on the software to write memos, letters, essays, books and his daily Gratitude Journal and to control his computer by voice. He says frankly, "Every estimate about how good accuracy you should get I find extremely annoying because it just makes you feel stupid and incompetent. I've never approached the kind of accuracy that's usually quoted—95 to 98 percent. That's just silly!"

To check your accuracy, read to your program from some written text for two or three minutes. Count the number of mistakes the program makes and divide by the total number of words you said. If, for example, your program makes 16 mistakes in 200 words, your error rate is eight percent (16 divided by 200). Your accuracy rate is 92 percent (184 correct words divided by 200). The error rate plus the accuracy rate totals 100 percent.

Peter Trier, Philosopher, Writer, & Disabled Rights Activist

"I would say DragonDictate puts down exactly what I want 75 percent of the time. Fifteen percent of the time, I can get the right word from the ten menu choices the program offers. Five percent of the time, if I say 'Spell mode,' I can type the changes in that way."

Being a philosopher committed to accuracy, Peter couldn't then fail to note that this actually adds up to 95 percent—still not too bad!

Peter's point is well taken, though. It's easy to feel incompetent and stupid if you're not achieving the results (you think) everyone else is. The point of these accuracy estimates is not to make you feel stupid but to give you guidelines. If your results are way off these estimates, it can be a sign that there are problems with your system. While your own manner of speaking is one important factor in accuracy, problems are often due to 'incompetent equipment,' or ill-trained software, not an incompetent you! Even if you find you can improve your speaking style, that's not a sign of your own drawbacks, just the computer's rigidity and need for consistent input.

Common Reasons for Low Accuracy

If you're getting less than 80 percent accuracy (more than two mistakes per sentence, on average), you might need to change your microphone or sound card, or make other adjustments to your computer.

For suggestions on troubleshooting low accuracy, see Chapter 9, Troubleshooting Common Problems.

Approaching the Speech Recognition Ideal

Like a problem-free romance, a system that delivers 100 percent accuracy is an unattainable ideal. You would have to:

▶ Always speak clearly and articulate each word.
▶ Sound exactly the same at all times and on all days.
▶ Have trained your program to recognize your voice exactly as it is at any given moment.
▶ Keep the microphone exactly the same distance from your mouth, in the same position.

▶ Use an ultra-high-fidelity microphone that transmits sounds exactly as you say them.

▶ Use a sound card that faithfully converts the microphone signal to digital form.

▶ Speak only words your program has in its vocabulary or has heard before.

▶ Compose only sentences similar to ones your program has heard before.

▶ Have the fastest available processor in your computer.

▶ Have at least 128 MB of RAM.

▶ Have a hard drive with enough free space.

▶ Work in a quiet room.

▶ Have no radio interference or electrical noise from power lines.

▶ Use the best available version of your speech recognition software.

▶ Run only your speech recognition program and no other programs.

Many of these items are impossible. No one's voice, for example, always sounds the same, and no microphone reproduces sounds 100 percent accurately. Other items are impractical. What fun is using your speech recognition program only in its own word processing window? It's more useful to dictate right into Word, Netscape, or your e-mail program. And only people who have a top-of-the line computer that's less than two weeks old have the fastest available processor.

Here's a guide to practical improvements, most of which don't require any money.

Improving Your Performance

One way you can improve your dictation accuracy is to improve the way you talk to your computer.

Speak Clearly

Speaking clearly and articulating each word is essential to getting high accuracy. The truism "garbage in, garbage out" applies here. The clearer your speech, the better your program will guess what you said. If you mumble and slur your words, you'll get errors everywhere, even if your computer is more powerful than NASA's.

See Chapter 3, Learning to Speak and Dictate to Your Computer, for tips on how to talk to your computer.

Keep the Microphone in the Same Position

Each time you use your program, try to place the microphone the same distance from your mouth. For most people, the best position for the microphone is about a thumb's width from the corner of your mouth.

If your computer adds unwanted short words to your dictation (like *a, in,* and *of*), the microphone may be picking up your breathing. Move the microphone closer to the corner of your mouth. If the mic is already at the corner of your mouth, move it about an inch farther away from your face. Also check that the microphone cord is not rustling against your clothes.

Teach the Program Your Style

Speech recognition software guesses what words you said from context as well as from the sound of your voice. If the words you say are similar to what you've said before, the program tends to guess what you say more accurately. The more context you give your program, the better the accuracy. Use the software's tools for building its vocabulary to teach it your writing style and what words you tend to use most often. You have two ways of doing this: Loading documents into the program that reflect your typical vocabulary; and entering new words by hand. Whichever method you use, entering the vocabulary words you commonly use will significantly improve the program's accuracy.

Retrain Your Program

People's voices change on different days and even within the same day. Speech recognition programs match your sounds to a computer model they make of your voice during initial enrollment (training). The more different your voice is from the model, the more mistakes the program will make.

You can't make your voice sound the same all the time, but with some programs you can re-enroll or retrain them, tuning your voice model to the way your voice sounds right now.

**Scott Hagen,
Vice-President, The Mechanics Bank**

Scott advises new users to be persistent. "Don't be thrown off by training the computer initially," he says. "The more you use it, the more familiar it becomes with your voice and style. Buy the software, buy a good training book and stick with it. I've only been using it for four months, and I'm very satisfied."

Scott Hagen did an end-run around around his hatred of typing by learning to use speech recognition to write.

Improving Your Hardware

Your program's mistakes are not all your fault. (Aren't you glad to hear that?) Just as when you talk to a person, mistakes and misunderstandings can occur because the reception isn't what it should be, even if you're being perfectly clear. Improving your computer's "ears"—and what's between them—can significantly improve both your dictation accuracy and speed.

Use a Good Microphone

All microphones distort the sound of your voice as it's transmitted to the computer, but some microphones work much better than others. The microphones included with most speech recognition software packages cost just a few dollars to manufacture and have limited fidelity. Most people get significantly better accuracy by switching to a higher-quality microphone. The Parrott-10 microphone, manufactured by VXI, sells for about $90 and is one of several good choices for a mic upgrade. Other manufacturers of high-quality microphones include Andrea Electronics, Philips, Sennheiser and Shure.

For details on a range of microphones, see "Microphones" in Chapter 8, Buyers Guide, page 125.

Headset microphones tend to give better accuracy than handheld microphones, which tend to move around more relative to your mouth. If your microphone moves around, your voice sounds less consistent.

Peter Trier, Philosopher, Writer & Disabled Rights Activist

Peter Trier offers a good tip for disabled users who, like him, have no hand use and need to use the microphone all day. "I use a music stand to hold my mic," he says, "because it's easily adjustable. It's too uncomfortable to wear the headset all day and night."

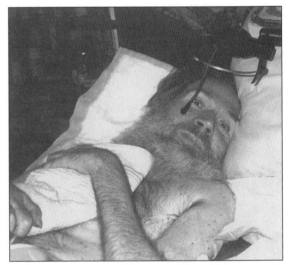

Peter Trier's body has become progressively more and more bed-bound, but his mind continues to roam freely, aided by Dragon-Dictate speech software.

Use a Good Sound Card

Your system's sound card is as important as your microphone in conveying a clear sound signal. Upgrading to a high-quality microphone will show no accuracy improvement if your sound card generates static or an insufficient signal level. As an alternative to changing your sound card, you can use one of the new microphones that connects by universal serial bus (USB). USB mics bypass the sound card and process the sound themselves.

Speech software programs have an automated setup process that helps insure the volume levels on your sound card are set correctly. If you are not achieving the results you would like, you can also test your card by ear, listening to your recorded speech through your computer's speakers.

Test Your Sound System

Here's a summary of steps you can take to improve your microphone and sound card combination:

1. Try your original equipment—the sound card included with your computer and the microphone included with your program. Use your program for at least a week, correcting errors as you go along and speaking clearly.

2. If you're not satisfied with your accuracy, use the Windows sound recorder to listen to how your voice sounds to your program. If your recorded voice sounds clear and free of static, the sound card and microphone are working fine. Otherwise, continue to step 3.

For more details on recording your speech and playing it back, see "Testing By Ear," page 153 (Chapter 9, Troubleshooting Common Problems).

3. If you have an integrated sound card, install a new sound card and go through your program's enrollment procedures again to set up your voice files with the new sound hardware.

4. If you're using a low-cost microphone (such as the microphones included with most programs), buy a better microphone.

For more detailed instructions on testing your sound system, see "Testing Your Sound System" page 153 (Chapter 9, Trouble-shooting Common Problems).

Have Sufficient Processor Speed, Memory, and Disk Space

Speech recognition is much more demanding of your computer's resources than most other applications you might regularly use—a testament to the complexity of human speech. Processor power boosts recognition performance, though it's less important than context and a clear speech signal. A faster processor (CPU) in your computer lets the software make more calculations in the same amount of time, so it can better hone in on what words you actually said. For optimal results, the speech software should not have to share processor power with any other programs running at the same time.

Your computer should also have enough memory (RAM) to hold your speech recognition program and any other programs running at the same time. If you are using only a dictation program with no other programs open, 64 MB of RAM should be sufficient. If you use your software as a command and control program, or use it to dictate with Word or other programs, as most people do, upgrading to 128 MB of RAM may improve recognition accuracy. Having more RAM enables your program to load more vocabulary into memory, and, with some programs, load more powerful recognition methods as well. Upgrading will also decrease your frustration by reducing some of the program's delays as you dictate and edit.

Hard disk space is relatively unimportant to program performance, as long as you have at about 500 MB free for the Windows operating system to use for temporary storage as you work. If your hard disk is more than about 5% fragmented, defragmenting your drive may improve your program's performance slightly.

You can defragment your disk by choosing Programs from the Windows Start menu, then choosing Accessories, System Tools, Disk Defragmenter. If you can't find the disk defragmenter this way, search the Windows help system. Utilities programs like Norton Utilities also include defragmenters. When you run the defragmentation program, be sure to close all other running programs except the operating system and the defragmenter.

Improve Speed with Proper Hardware

On all systems, there's a delay between when you speak and when your program types out what you said. The program uses this delay time, plus the time when you're talking, to recognize your speech. The faster your processor, the shorter the delay. Using a CPU that's 400 MHz or faster reduces the delay to almost nothing, and your speech appears about as rapidly as you talk.

How Much Difference Can Your System Make?

In Chapter 2, you "met" the systems of a few of our profiled users. Kristin Barendsen uses one of the older systems of all our profiled users: A PC with a Pentium 166 MHz processor, 96 MB RAM, and a relatively small 1.2 gigabyte hard drive. She also uses a SoundBlaster sound card and the VXI Parrott-10 mic that came with her speech recognition program. She suspects she would get better performance with a faster system.

Scott Hagen, vice-president of The Mechanic's Bank, on the other hand, just recently bought his system and bought the fastest processor currently available—a 500 MHz Pentium III chip. His system has 128 MB of RAM and a Turtle Beach sound card. He has used his speech recognition program on another, slower system and the difference is noticeable enough that he now works exclusively on the new machine. He says that his program accepted dictation "almost immediately" and it took him only a few days to become familiar with the main program commands.

User Donald Winiecki, who you'll hear more about later in this chapter, has one of the more unique systems among our profiled users. He has an Olympus D-1000 recorder that he uses with ViaVoice. The recorder saves voice files on a PCMCIA card, a small card the size of a credit card that he slides into an adapter for his Pentium 133 MHz notebook computer. He then puts his recorder speech file on a Zip disk or e-mails it to his office, where he uses a Pentium 200MHz system running VaVoice software to transcribe it.

Improving Your Hardware's Performance

Even if you have an older system that doesn't match the ideal specifications recommended in this book, you can still get more out of what you have by taking a few simple steps.

Reduce Background Noise

Speech recognition programs perform best in a quiet room. In a noisy office, accuracy will decrease slightly, though the software will still work. For best results, train (or retrain) your voice files in the same environment as you'll be dictating.

Donald Winiecki, Professor

Don Winiecki uses his recorder in a number of different locations. "My original enrollment was in a very quiet environment. Now, if I dictate at home and my dog barks, or when classes are changing and there's a din in the hall, recognition goes down.

"The program manual says you can perform multiple enrollments for different environments. I should really enroll during a class change so the machine gets used to the background noise. Because I've had good luck with it right out of the gate, I'm afraid I'm a bit spoiled though."

If a consistent background noise like an air conditioner or fan interferes with good recognition, consider a microphone with active noise cancellation. This type of mic removes background noise from the sound of your voice, delivering a clear speech signal to the computer.

See the section on microphones in Chapter 8, Buyers Guide, for descriptions of several noise canceling mics and manufacturer contact information.

Eliminate Electrical Interference

In some cases, noise in a building's electrical wiring will generate static in your computer's sound card. Few desktop users encounter this problem; it's mostly limited to laptops, where the power source and sound card are more likely to be crammed together. If your laptop is performing slowly or inaccurately, try unplugging it and operating only from battery power to eliminate possible interference from the building wiring. A USB microphone, which bypasses the computer's sound card, can also be an effective solution.

Improving Your Software

Improvements in speech recognition software are coming fast and furiously, and most manufacturers offer new versions of their programs every six to nine months. When your program is running, choose the About command from its Help menu and check the version number of your program. Are you using the most current version? If your program is a year old or more, you can be pretty sure the answer is *no*. Visit the manufacturer's Web site to find out what the most current version might be. You can also call your local computer software store to ask.

If you don't have the most current version, consider upgrading. An upgrade costs less than the original program. While you may need to retrain your software, users typically find the improvement in accuracy and ease of use well worth the trouble and small cost of upgrading.

Using Speech Recognition with Other Software

When dictating into your dictation program's word processing window with no other programs running, your computer's power is dedicated to processing your speech. If other programs are also open, or if you're dictating into another program, your computer must divide its processing power between processing your speech and other tasks. Some programs use more computing resources than others. WordPad and Eudora, for example, take little processing power, so dictating into these programs, or using your speech recognition software while these programs are open, will not decrease your program's accuracy or speed significantly. Microsoft Word, however, uses a great deal of system resources, and dictating into Word can be slower than dictating into your speech recognition program directly.

Some programs that use system resources run in the background, without appearing in an on–screen window. Virus software and "reminder" alarm clock programs are among the programs in this category. To find and remove software running in the background, see "Software Conflicts" on page 153 (Chapter 9, Trouble-shooting Common Problems).

Achieving Better Accuracy with a Recorder

Transcribing from a recorder tends to be less accurate than dictating directly into the computer for several reasons.

- ▶ The built-in microphone in the recorder may be lower quality than the headset microphone you use for dictation directly to the computer.
- ▶ Like using a handheld microphone, using a handheld recorder keeps the microphone in a less consistent place from your mouth than does a headset microphone.
- ▶ Minicassette recorders and other analog models lose sound information in both recording and playback. They record only part of your voice, then play back only part of what they record to be processed by the sound card. (Digital recorders that digitally transfer sound do not have this limitation. They also record only part of your voice, but they bypass the sound card, sending the digital recording file directly to the speech recognition program for transcription.)

▶ Using a recorder, people more often mumble and slur their words. They forget they are talking for a computer to transcribe.

To get the best accuracy from a recorder, use an external microphone if your recorder's built–in microphone has limited fidelity. Nearly all recorders allow you to plug in an external mic to replace the unit's built-in one. Using a headset microphone is best, since it keeps the mic at a constant distance from your mouth. Try using the headset mic included with your speech software.

Most people don't want to carry around a headset microphone with their recorder, even if it will give them better accuracy. "Stalk" microphones are also available. These stick out a inch or two from the recorder like a small mushroom.

For more information on stalk microphones, see the "Microphones" section of Chapter 8, Buyers Guide, page 125.

If you're using the recorder's built-in mic, keep it a consistent distance from your mouth. It should be at the corner of your mouth, about an inch away. See the instructions included with your recorder or experiment to find the best distance.

Speaking clearly will improve transcription accuracy no matter what recorder you have. Remember that you're talking for a computer, not a person. Speak clearly, speak with energy and pronounce each word.

Donald Winiecki, **Professor**

Don Winiecki, Ed.D., is an assistant professor at Boise State University in Idaho, one of the more rural states in the country. He teaches traditional on-campus classes but to make it easier for remote students to study, he also teaches online classes in Boise State's asynchronous distance learning program.

"I need to adapt my classroom lecture notes and materials into text that I can post online for my distance students," he explains.

Don has found that using a recorder with speech recognition software "allows me to bridge these two teaching situations... It's made what I do more comfortable & manageable. I spend less time on my notes so I can spend more time on research."

He's developed his own unique work style. "As I'm rehearsing my lectures or discussing things with my graduate students, I run my recorder, an Olympus D-1000 recorder that includes a version of ViaVoice. I then run my practice lecture and our discussions through ViaVoice, take pieces of the transcripts and then piece them together to create my online notes." Remarkably, he says he even gets reasonably good accuracy when ViaVoice transcribes his graduate assistant's voice, even though she has never enrolled in ViaVoice.

Backing Up Speech Files

It's important to back up your speech files regularly. As you use your program, it adapts to your voice and learns your personal added words. Making regular backups, perhaps every week, saves having to start from scratch should something happen to your computer (and believe me, sometime, it will).

Check your program's documentation to see if it makes an automatic backup of your speech files. You may need to select an option in a dialog box to turn this automatic backup feature on, or it may automatically be selected the first time you start up your program.

You should also save a backup of your voice files on a tape or Zip drive as well, so you can store a backup away from your computer. If your computer is on an office network, you may be able to copy your speech files to the server or storage area on your network, where it will be safely backed up by your company's information systems staff.

A Suggested Backup System

There are two types of computer users: those who have lost data and those who haven't yet. We all know that backing up is important, but many of us avoid it because it's a hassle. After years of error and trial I've hit upon a system that's simple enough that I actually do it. Maybe it will work for you too.

Preparing for Backup

Keep all documents to be backed up in one folder, with subfolders. For example, keep your files in the "My Documents" folder, inside subfolders for business, personal, and other categories meaningful to you. Avoid storing files with the application that created them (Word files with the Word program, Excel files with Excel) because this makes backing up less convenient. Some applications, like e-mail programs, require that the files you create be stored with the application. However, for files you can choose where to place, place them all within the same folder.

Buy a Zip or recordable CD-ROM drive. Tape drives tend to be slow and cumbersome.

Read your speech recognition program's documentation (or search the online Help file) to find out where the program stores your speech files.

Use the backup software that came with your drive to select the folders and files to back up. Include the "My Documents" folder, your program's voice files, and your e-mail and other files that couldn't be saved into the "My Documents" folder. Set your backup program on Verify to have the computer double-check each backup for accuracy. Save these settings.

Prepare three sets of backup disks. Depending on how many files you have, you may need three or more disks in each set. Label the disks "set A disk 1," "set A disk 2," and so on.

Keeping a Weekly Routine

Run a backup using the settings you created in the backup software. If you're at work, store the backup disk set you just created safely at home, and return the old backup disks from home to work to reuse. Take the newest set somewhere apart from your computer (in this example, home, or to a safe deposit box) and bring the oldest set back home to be reused. The three disk sets you created should rotate. One set should always be at home, one at work, and the third in transit.

Ensuring Additional Backup Security

For more protection against losing data, make an additional set of backup disks every three months and store them in a safe deposit box or with a friend. If something happens to your computer or to your weekly backups, you'll have these disks to fall back on.

To verify that your backup system is working, use the Retrieve or Restore function in your backup software to recover an old file from a backup set. Do this at least every three months.

Building Your Program's Vocabulary

While each of the four major programs use different combinations of technology, they all use statistical models of which words tend to go together and which words you use most often. These statistical models have been created by analyzing general business writing because that's what the largest number of users are likely to need. The programs therefore work best out of the box when you dictate business letters, memos and other documents of similar language. If you dictate a laboratory report or a poem, your program will tend to make more errors.

For best accuracy, you need to train the program in your particular vocabulary. One way you can do this is to show your program samples of the types of documents you write and the words you use most often. Most program editions have a vocabulary building tool that lets your program learn your writing style.

Choose documents typical of those you normally dictate. If you tend to write memos, letters and reports, find a few representative samples of each. Your program will use these files as a guide to the type of writing it expects to hear.

Kristin Barendsen, Writer & Editor

Kristin Barendsen writes and edits a wide range of documents, ranging from marketing literature, Web content and computer documentation to travel essays and fiction. After being stricken with a severe case of RSI that left her on disability for a year, Kristin discovered speech recognition software, which has enabled her to return to work. She says, "NaturallySpeaking is programmed to do better in the more straightfor-

ward tasks. I find it doesn't do as well with slang in e-mails, humor and other more unusual usages.

"I don't really have just one vocabulary. NaturallySpeaking does pretty well in recognizing the technical language. But then I also write articles about topics like yoga and trekking in Nepal that use terms the program isn't used to. I also try to use the language in slightly unusual ways for artistic purposes and the program has a hard time with that."

Kristin finds, though, that if she takes the time to train the program in her vocabulary, her accuracy improves. "Using this software is almost like being in a relationship, a marriage. You have to keep putting in the time to make things work. You have to stick to it. When I build time for that into my work schedule, it pays off tremendously!"

How Vocabulary Builders Improve Accuracy

The vocabulary builder tool in your speech recognition program analyzes your writing to discover what are your most commonly used words and phrases. This analysis changes the program's expectations about how often you say different words and phrases. For example, if you're a teacher who often uses the word "grades," your program will be much less likely after processing to mistakenly type "graves." In short, you're teaching the program your writing style.

The vocabulary builder tool also finds words the program has never seen before. It lists these words for you and asks if you'd like to add any of them to the program's vocabulary.

Adding Specialized Vocabularies

If you use a specialized professional terminology, you may be able to purchase an add-on vocabulary or a special professional edition that already contains an appropriate vocabulary. The additional cost is well worth the increase in accuracy the program has right out of the box, as well as worth the correction and vocabulary-building time you save.

At the moment, the greatest number of add-on vocabularies are available for the medical and legal fields. However, you can find programs and add-ons that address other areas—for example, L&H has a Voice Xpress edition for safety professionals.

Bruce MacLeod, Securities Lawyer

Bruce has pronounced ideas about how to make the software work well. "I didn't buy the legal edition of the program I use. I just use the basic professional version. The vocabulary used in my area of law is so specialized that it wouldn't be reflected in the legal edition's vocabulary."

He stresses the importance of knowing the right time and strategy for correcting. "You have to learn when you just dictate over the word versus when you type in the word, and when you go through the vocabulary editor routine. I don't think the importance of the vocabulary editor and vocabulary builder are understood very well by most users. The builder is important. You don't get decent recognition if you don't run it. The vocabulary editor is important in maybe only ten percent of the training that you do, but there are certain situations in which it's the only effective way." The vocabulary editor tool in each program lets you view all the words in your program's vocabulary and directly train the ones you want.

Training Misrecognized Words and Commands

Sometimes speech software will persistently misrecognize a word, phrase or command. If this happens, take advantage of your program's training features to retrain it. Training a word involves typing or spelling the word, then saying it so the computer can learn it better. Like correcting the computer's transcription errors, training consistently misrecognized words is key to achieving top accuracy.

5

Keeping Healthy While Computing

This chapter introduces you to the basics of keeping healthy while computing. As someone with RSI, I had to learn this information the hard way—through pain and the frustration of being unable to work as I wanted. Don't learn the way I did! Taking care of yourself and setting up your workstation properly now will pay big dividends in improved comfort and better health long into the future.

Since becoming a consultant on speech recognition, I have continued to learn about ergonomics from a number of leading experts in the field. I've also read widely and learned from my experience helping users set up comfortable speech recognition workstations. This chapter condenses my experience into practical tips for the everyday user of speech programs.

The Three Keys to Healthy Computing

The three keys to healthy computing by voice are simple to state but take time and attention to carry out.

Cultivate Calmness

The best way to stay healthy at your computer is to stay relaxed and change posture frequently. Many of us tense up around computers. Cultivating calmness and variety will make your body feel good.

Choose the Right Equipment

Equally important is choosing the right equipment and positioning it to fit your body. Your keyboard, mouse, monitor and chair should be set up to cause minimal strain.

Care for Your Voice

Voice care is also vital. Radio announcers and disc jockeys depend on their voices for their livelihood. Using speech recognition, you're also depending on your voice. Not surprisingly, speech therapists report that people who use speech recognition regularly but who do not properly care for their voice can injure their vocal cords. So don't wait for your voice to start showing the strain—work right from the beginning.

Maintaining Good Ergonomics and Posture

Good ergonomics—setting up your equipment to properly fit your body—is essential for healthy computing. Adjusting your monitor or keyboard even an inch or two can make a big difference by reducing tension in your neck, shoulders, and hands. One of the most common problem with people's workstations is that the keyboard and mouse are too high. Deidre Rogers, a nurse and ergonomics specialist from the ergonomics consulting firm Ergovera, observes that, "Most people don't realize that just two hours a day of having your keyboard too high may lead to soft tissue injury."

If you are experiencing pain, discomfort or any other problems that seem to result from working with your computer, you should immediately seek professional medical attention.

When adjusting your workstation, comfort should be your main guide. The suggestions that follow work for many people. Ergonomics is a young field, however, and research is ongoing. Experts do not always agree about the causes of problems or the best solutions. Since pain is a later sign of injury, you certainly don't want to wait until you feel pain before you change your work style. However, your own body ultimately signals the best arrangement for your workstation.

Setting Up for Speech Recognition

A good ergonomic setup for speech recognition is basically the same as a good setup for typing. Speech recognition users, though, have more flexibility to move, shift positions and stretch while dictating. Figure 5-1 shows an example of a well-designed workstation.

Setting the Proper Chair Height

Set your chair height so that your feet can be flat on the ground and your hips are an inch or two above your knees. You don't have to keep your feet on the ground while working, however, so feel free to cross your legs or straighten your knees.

You also want to have your chair high enough to spread your weight between your legs and your buttocks, so your weight is not all on your lower back.

Figure 5-1

A well-designed workstation combines the right equipment set at the right height for your height and body type.

If the chair is the proper height, your body weight will be supported partly by your feet but mostly by the chair seat and backrest. If you are short and find your legs don't reach the ground, you should consider a footstool (or just try a telephone book or two stacked under your desk).

Footstools do limit the amount your feet can move, though. With a footstool, "the feet have only one place to be, and leg postures are limited. It's better to get the chair down to the right level," says Chris Grant, Ph.D., of the consulting firm F-One Ergonomics. If people work at a workstation where they frequently move the chair between work areas, people may use the footrest erratically, or the footrest and chair combination may be at the wrong height for some of the work surfaces.

Sitting Correctly

When sitting, it's best for your hip angle—the angle your thighs make with your torso—to be as wide as possible, certainly more than 90 degrees and even as wide as 130 degrees. This requires that your chair seat be high enough so that your hips are above your knees. For greatest comfort, your chair seat should tilt forward rather than remaining flat.

Grant describes how opening the hip angle benefits the body: "When the hips are straightened, the vertebrae are aligned with each other in a way that reduces and evens out pressure on the intervertebral discs." (These discs are the spongy stuff that sits like pads between your backbones.)

Sitting with the legs open is good but a forward tilt to the chair is also key, as it distributes the weight more evenly between the legs and back and also encourages movement. Sitting in the "athletic position"—that is, upright in a position of readiness to move, with feet on the floor and weight spread evenly across the legs—is a sitting posture that works well for many people.

What If You Stand?

Many people have shifted to standing desks trying to avoid the problems of bad chairs and workstation design. Not surprisingly, the result for many is that they now have problems with their feet. While standing is not a bad solution, the key, once again, is to vary your posture and keep moving throughout the day. Shifting back and forth between sitting and standing is one option.

If you stand, make sure your monitor is at a proper height. You can buy a sturdy adjustable monitor stand like the one in use in Figure 5-2 that enables you to easily adjust your monitor's height up and down without strain.

Setting the Correct Keyboard Height

The keyboard should be at elbow height or lower. If the keyboard is at ideal height, the angle of your elbows while typing should be slightly more open than 90 degrees. The mouse or other pointing device should be at the same height as the keyboard and as close to the keyboard as possible.

Make sure that your wrists are straight, regardless of keyboard height. Your hand should be in the same line as the forearm, rather than bent up or forward. Incorrect wrist posture can cause fatigue or nerve damage in the entire area below the elbow.

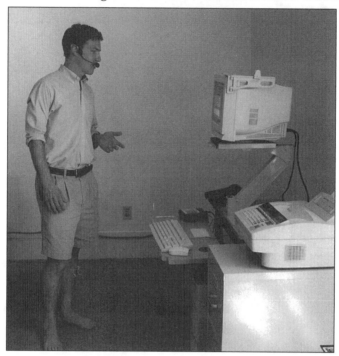

Figure 5-2

Chris Carrigg often likes to dictate while roaming, which allows him to stay in motion and out of pain. With his new wireless headset, he's not held back

Setting the Correct Monitor Height

The highest your monitor should be is with the top of the screen at eye level, or an inch or two below eye level. The best height depends partly on the programs you use most often. If you run programs with mid-screen viewing windows, you may want to raise your monitor a bit higher. With this positioning, you can look straight ahead to see the first line of type in your document, and read the rest of the screen by moving your eyes down—moving the whole head is not necessary. (Look back to Figure 5-1 and ahead to Figure 5-7 for examples of monitors set to proper height.) If you find that this height is uncomfortable for your neck, make the monitor lower. Experimenting with a lower monitor height is worth trying if you tend to have pain in your upper back, neck or shoulders. Also make sure that no light sources are reflected in the monitor. If there are windows in the same room as the computer, it's usually best to place the monitor at a right angle (perpendicular) to the windows to reduce reflections.

Finding the Right Arm and Hand Position

In order to avoid injury, you should try to position yourself so your hand and arm position match as closely as possible their position when you are standing in a "neutral" position with your arms at your side (see Figure 5-3). To stand in a neutral position, stand comfortably and naturally with your weight spread evenly over both feet. When you are in neutral position, typically your elbow is partially flexed, your fingers curl, and your arms roll outward from your shoulder so your palms are facing your thighs. This flex, curl and roll is the natural tension of your body's tendons.

Then, if you work in a chair at a keyboard, sit at your keyboard maintaining your arms in their neutral position, as Chris does in Figure 5-4.

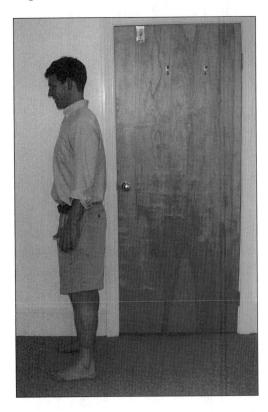

Figure 5-3

Start from a neutral position in which you are alert but at rest, without unnatural tension in any of your body parts.

Keeping your arms in neutral position and your elbows close to your side, raise your arms until your hands are over the keyboard in position to type. Rotate your wrists and hands inwards so your fingers meet the keys; however, your arms should still be rotated outwards slightly, as they are in your neutral position also. The goal is to position your hands so you don't feel any unnatural tension in your forearms. You can see an example of a good position in Figure 5-5. (Keep in mind though, that everyone's body is different. Let your body be your guide.)

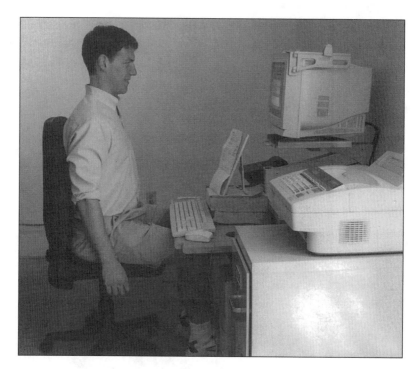

Figure 5-4

Start with your arms in a neutral position like this when you sit at the keyboard, and then move them into typing position.

I bet that you have seen many more people sitting at their workstations who look like Figure 5-6—which is a fine visual catalog of what *not* to do!

Figure 5-5

Here's an example of a good workstation setup and keyboard position. Note how Chris has placed the document on a document stand directly in front of him so he doesn't need to crane his neck to read it.

Figure 5-6

This character is on the road to early retirement from RSI! What's wrong with this picture? Here's a short list: head jutting forward; weight placed entirely on the lower back, not spread onto the feet and legs; shoulders slumped forward; wrists bent; monitor too high; head pushed forward; chest and spine collapsed; body positioned at an angle to the computer.

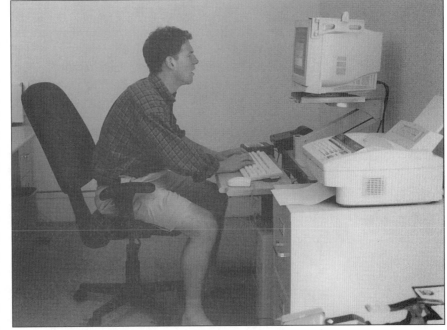

Avoiding Injury by Conventional Wisdom

Computers, keyboards and RSI have been around for some years now—long enough so that there's conventional wisdom that tells you how to best work and configure your workspace to avoid injury. A lot of this conventional wisdom seems like common sense but turned out to be useless or even harmful when ergonomics experts took a closer look.

Here are a few key recommendations for avoiding injury by conventional wisdom.

▶ **Don't wait until you feel pain to change your working ways.**
Many people think that their work habits are fine if they're not feeling chronic pain. That's not true. Pain is a late sign of problems. By the time you feel pain, you may already have serious injuries that will take a long time to heal. Optimize your work setup before pain starts.

▶ **Take frequent, short breaks, not a long break every few hours.**
The key to maintaining your health is maintaining variety in your posture, activity and mood. You're better off taking mini-breaks of even thirty seconds or a minute than waiting an hour before stretching.

▶ **Avoid using footrests if there's an alternative.**
While footrests are better than leaving your legs dangling above the floor, they are distinctly second best to positioning yourself so you can rest your feet on the floor.

Here are a few tips if you are already feeling discomfort:

▶ **Don't overuse anti-inflammatory drugs.**
Too many people take their cue from sports superstars. They take anti-inflammatory drugs on a regular basis and just keep on working. These drugs mask your symptoms without solving the problem, however. Pain is your body's warning signal that you've gone too far. Dulling your pain and inflammation with drugs is like closing your eyes in front of a fire: The fire doesn't go away and it burns just as hot; you just don't see it anymore. If you keep working under the same conditions, you risk more serious and lasting injury.

▶ **If you wear wrist splints, do so only when resting, not when typing.**
Wearing restrictive splints for extended periods of time while working may lead to muscle wasting and decreased circulation.

Know Thyself—and Thy Body

Developing self-awareness of both body and spirit is a key to staying healthy while computing.

Too many of us have never learned to read our bodies' signals, or have learned to ignore our bodies altogether. Most of us who work in offices, factories, and other constrained environments move and use our muscles in ways that are not ideal, decreasing our comfort and contributing to the chances of becoming injured. Our bodies tell us when we're straining ourselves and plea with us to stop and rest, but too often we accept symptoms like back pain and stiffness, sore necks, mild tingling, and tired hands and wrists as normal. Instead of reading our bodies signals, we tune them out. That's what my business manager, Chris Carrigg, did. He says, "I just thought the burning sensation and pain in my shoulders and back were normal adult aches and pains. I didn't pay attention." The result? Chris developed RSI that left him seriously disabled and has taken years to overcome.

Regular exercise brings better body awareness as it also brings calmness and (after the first few weeks!) more energy. The health benefits of all exercise are plentiful and well documented. Becoming more tuned-in to your body and its signals is one more reason to make exercise time.

Any good body movement and awareness program, such as the Alexander technique or Feldenkreiss, can also help you reconnect with your body and learn to move in a more natural way that matches your body's needs. Ergonomics specialist Rogers successfully uses biofeedback techniques with her clients as well.

Your body is, of course, connected to your emotions and spirit. People with different personalities react differently to workplace stress and workload. Are you a go-getter in the morning who hates to be trapped at the computer when you're raring to go? Or are you a quiet type who gets stressed in meetings and finds yourself huddled over your keyboard after a tense meeting? Pay attention to how your personality and reactions to your work environment affect your posture and attitude as you work at the computer. Knowing your own patterns and planning your workday to match your personality and work style will help you lessen the strain you place on your body.

Solutions to Common Workspace Problems

Because of the standard design of desks, chairs and computers, people encounter common problems in adjusting their workspaces for healthy computing. The solutions for these problems don't have to be expensive. Some of these inexpensive solutions are described below.

Hopefully, as consumers and businesses begin to wake up to the seriousness of RSI and furniture companies change their designs to better accommodate our bodies, such piecemeal solutions will no longer be needed.

Lowering Your Keyboard

If your monitor and keyboard are both sitting on the desktop, the keyboard is probably way too high.

Lowering the height of the keyboard usually requires installing a keyboard tray. Fully adjustable keyboard trays can run $200 or more. Less expensive, less adjustable models from Rubbermaid and other manufacturers are available from office supply stores. Look for a tray with room for the mouse as well as the keyboard and make sure the angle of the keyboard can be adjusted both backward and forwards so you can find the most comfortable position. Most models attach to the underside of the desk with screws.

Though expensive, a good keyboard tray can make a big difference in comfort and preventing injury. In the meantime, try typing with the keyboard on your lap. This is not a good long-term solution because it prevents you from moving around, but working with the keyboard on your lap can help you determine if lowering the keyboard will be more comfortable for you.

You can also buy workstations designed for use with computers that come in two pieces (one for keyboard, one for monitor) or have a built-in keyboard tray. You can see the two-piece workstation Kristin Barendsen uses in Figure 5-7.

Even for people who use speech recognition, keyboard height is important. Most speech recognition users find themselves typing at times.

Figure 5-7

Kristin Barendsen uses a two-piece workstation that enables her to lower her keyboard almost to lap level while keeping her monitor at proper height. Note how the monitor is slightly lower than her eye level.

Raising Your Chair Height

If your desk cannot accommodate a keyboard tray, a compromise solution is raising your chair height so that your elbow angle is a bit more open than 90 degrees. At this chair height, your feet may dangle off the ground—you'll need a footrest so you can place your feet on a flat surface. Adjustable footrests are available, but a sturdy box of the right height works well too. As noted in an earlier section, though, footrests are less than ideal because they limit your leg posture. If you use a footrest remember to move your feet and legs frequently.

Overcoming Laptop Limitations

Laptop computers, unmodified, are ergonomically terrible. Placed on a table or desk, the keyboard is too high, the monitor is too low and the pointing devices are small and awkward to use. Have an external monitor, keyboard, and mouse at each location you use the computer frequently (say, home and office). If this is not possible, at least have an external keyboard at each location. Standard keyboards cost $25 or less. Put the laptop on a monitor stand, box, or stack of paper so that the top of the laptop screen is at eye level or lower. Use the external keyboard, and an external mouse, in a keyboard tray. If you don't have a keyboard tray, try using the keyboard on your lap.

Consulting the Experts

If you work in an office or other organization where many people use computers, your organization may benefit from hiring an ergonomics consultant to evaluate your workplace and recommend a comprehensive solution to RSI hazards. Although this might sound like an expensive proposition, the Occupational Safety and Health Administration (OSHA) estimates that at least $20 billion a year is lost to business and industry due to RSI—not to mention the thousands of lives that are permanently altered because of this wholly preventable disorder.

Taking Speech Recognition into Account

Although you follow the same principles to create healthy workstations for typing and speech recognition, there are some strain issues specific to using speech recognition. "I've seen people use some really awkward postures," says consultant Rogers, "as they stoop over to see their screen as they dictate." To avoid this, increase the fonts in your program to a large size so you don't need to lean forward and squint.

Many people experience stress when first starting to use speech recognition software as they watch the program make mistakes. When you are feeling more stress, you tend to tense your muscles. Breathe deeply and relax your upper body muscles, and remember that the computer's mistakes are part of the normal process of working by voice. Looking away from the screen and closing your eyes while dictating also help reduce stress.

Buying the Right Equipment

Creating a comfortable workstation is well worth an investment of time and money. You probably already have a chair, keyboard and mouse—but do they help or hurt your body?

Try Before You Buy

Equipment choices are quite personal: One person's dreamy comfort is another's tortured hell. If you can, try several devices—over a few days, if possible—and choose based on comfort. Consultant Rogers suggests that businesses consider setting up a lab where employees can go and try different types of equipment. If you're an individual user, go to your local computer or office equipment store. Big computer superstores usually don't offer much sales help, but they do at least place many different models of keyboards, mice, and office chairs on display so you can feel and try them to make an initial judgment about designs that might work for you.

Chairs

A comfortable, adjustable office chair lasts many years and can prevent pain and increase comfort. Look for a chair with these characteristics:

- ▶ Adjusts in height.
- ▶ Swivels.
- ▶ Has a tilting back.
- ▶ Has a tilting seat.

If you prefer using a chair with arms, be sure to get a chair with adjustable arms as well.

Adjustments let you vary your posture as you work so you're not stuck in a fixed position all the time. Notes ergonomics expert Grant, "posture change seems to be as important as posture correctness" in preventing RSI. Discs in the spine lose fluid during the day because of the weight that they carry. "Changing your posture during the days appears to help pump fluid back into these discs."

Chris Carrigg favors chairs that encourage movement by design, such as saddle-shaped chairs by Hag that are meant only for temporary resting, not reclining.

Besides choosing the right type of chair, you should also choose a chair that fits you properly. The seat base should provide support for your upper thighs, as well as back, but should not be so long in its depth so that it presses against your upper calf.

Your seat should have a forward seat tilt, which both helps move some of your weight onto your legs and encourages movement. It also straightens your upper back and prevents shortening of your neck and upper back muscles.

The back of the chair should extend high enough to support the upper part of your back and low enough to support your lower back.

Take your body size and type into account as well. Many chairs are not well designed for narrow shouldered people, who need a smaller chair back. The smaller chair back gives good lumbar support and allows greater upper extremity movement. Most chairs are also not well designed for smaller people (under 5"4') or extremely tall and big people (over 6" and/or heavier than 275 lbs.). If you fall into one of these categories, you may need to special order a chair rather than buy one off the showroom floor.

Of all your office furniture, the chair may be the most important in maintaining your health, but you have no way of knowing if a chair is right for you in the showroom. There's no such thing as a chair that works for everyone because everyone's body is different. Ideally, you should try out a chair for a few days. If you have a choice, you should definitely buy a chair from a company that gives you a trial period or a money-back guarantee.

Keyboards

The many available alternatives to a traditional flat keyboard offer different shapes and key configurations. Manufacturers claim that typing on their keyboards strains the hands less than the traditional flat keyboard. Ergonomics experts express skepticism about many of these claims and emphasize that each person's body and needs are different.

The most common ergonomic feature is a split, angled arrangement that aims keys toward your elbows, but ergonomists have pointed out that this particular design addresses a problem that really isn't very important in most cases. Experts also say that it isn't only the angle at which you type which is important, but also the force with which you strike the keys. If you really pound the keyboard, you may experience problems regardless of the keyboard you use.

One key to choosing a well fitting keyboard is knowing your body type. Many people of greater girth find that split-keyboards work best. According to consultant Rogers, current research suggests people with narrow shoulders may be better off using a shorter width keyboard (with the numeric ten-key pad missing), so the mouse can be placed closer to the person's midline. This helps reduce extended reaching for the mouse, which can lead to muscle fatigue and possibly injury.

Many speech recognition users find that they type relatively little and do fine with standard keyboards.

The bottom line is, take short, frequent breaks during your work and rest your hands. This is more healthy than constant work on any alternative keyboard. If you do buy a keyboard with an alternative design, try before you buy. If you're unable to find what you need on display in a store, some companies will let you take a device home for a trial period or allow you to return it if you're not satisfied.

Mice and Other Pointing Devices

Many users report that pressing the mouse button eventually causes more discomfort than either moving the mouse or typing. Try to keep the natural shape of your hand as you curl your fingers or hand around your pointing device and use your whole hand to press the mouse buttons, not just your forefinger. This lessens the use of the tendons in your forearms. Using your software's Ctrl shortcut keys and other available keyboard shortcuts is also an excellent way to reduce mouse use.

If you prefer a traditional mouse, find one that requires a light touch on its mouse buttons. Many mice now also come with thumb buttons and programs that enable you to customize your assignments so you can, for example, assign a button to execute a double-click with only a single click from you. (Be careful not to overuse your thumb, however.) You can also get mice with small scroll wheels in the middle that scroll your screen, avoiding some of the rolling and clicking that's otherwise required. Other pointing devices available include:

Figure 5-8

The Kensington Turbo Mouse Trackball is one of the most popular trackballs currently available. The ball is large enough so you can rest your entire palm on it.

Figure 5-9

The Microsoft Easy Ball features a super large trackball that works well for many people with limited motor control.

Trackballs. Many trackballs feature a ball the size of a pool ball set in a recessed box. To move the pointer, roll the ball with your fingertips or palm. To click, press buttons, like a mouse. Kensington makes a popular trackball of this type, shown in Figure 5-8. Another manufacturer, Logitech, makes trackballs with a walnut-sized ball you roll with your thumb. The Microsoft EasyBall (shown in Figure 5-9), designed for children, is a bright yellow trackball a bit larger than a grapefruit. Some adults with limited hand use prefer this device.

Touch pads. Touch pads, pressure-sensitive rectangles, are found on many laptops. They are available as external pointing devices for desktops as well or are built into some keyboards. Slide one finger on the pad to move the pointer. Click by gently tapping your finger on the pad. This is the only type of pointing device that doesn't necessarily require pressing buttons to click—instead you tap on the pad with a very light touch. Glidepoint pads from Cirque, such as their Power Cat model (shown in Figure 5-10), work especially well. (Note that some touchpads do come with buttons you need to click, so be sure you check before you buy.)

Foot mouse. To use the No-Hands Mouse from Hunter Digital, rest your feet atop its two oval pedals. Swivel one foot to move the pointer, and use your other foot to click. This pointing device, shown in Figure 5-11, is a viable option for people with little or no hand use. People who are able to use a hand-operated device tend to find the foot mouse cumbersome.

Figure 5-10

With a touchpad, slide your finger on the pad to move the onscreen pointer and tap gently on the pad to click.

Figure 5-11

This No-Hands mouse is a good choice for people with limited or no use of their hands.

Figure 5-12

The Goldtouch mouse was developed by a movement expert who developed RSI.

Foot control pedals. Step-On-It pedals from Bilbo Innovations let you press keys, enter key sequences or click the mouse by pressing one of three pedals. You still need a mouse or other pointing device to move the cursor. For greatest comfort, keep your legs and feet relaxed when using these devices.

No single tool will prevent RSI or stop RSI symptoms. The most important things are for you to vary the work your muscles do, take regular breaks, and stretch. Using more than one kind of input device and switching back and forth between them might be better than just using one device, regardless of its design. Any computer running Windows 98 that has a USB (Universal Serial Bus) port enables you to connect several different input devices at the same time so you can switch back and forth during one work session without restarting your computer.

Touchpads and trackballs don't solve the major problem with pointing devices, which is overuse of the delicate, small muscles and tendons of the hands and arms. Rogers recommends using pointing devices that enable you to use your bigger, stronger muscles. She recommends the Kensington Orbit and the Goldtouch mouse (see Figure 5-12), which was designed by a kinesiologist who developed RSI. As yet, few such pointing devices exist, but hopefully manufacturers will soon catch up to the latest ergonomic wisdom.

Maintaining Good Vocal Health

Some people experience vocal strain when using speech recognition software. Like an athlete stretching before a run, you can take preventative measures to maintain good vocal health.

Speak Normally Following These Guidelines

Here's what to do to speak in a healthy manner:

▶ Speak in a relaxed matter, approximating your normal flow of speech.

▶ Use pitch and inflection. There's no need to speak in a monotone. You'll put much more energy into your voice this way, which is healthier for you.

▶ Speaking well has an open feeling to it, like the feeling inside right before a yawn. This open sense, which has been described as an "inner smile," makes for sound, comfortable speaking.

▶ Breathe with the diaphragm, rather than in the chest, supporting your voice.

Exercise: Notice Your Breathing

Put your hand on your belly. If you're breathing through your diaphragm, your hand will rise (your belly will expand) as you inhale. As you exhale, your hand will fall. Breathing this way may take some practice, but it's well worth getting into the habit.

If you're breathing from the chest, your chest will rise and fall instead of your belly.

Vary Your Gestures and Posture

If you typically make hand gestures as you speak to other people in person, go ahead and make those gestures at the computer. Your voice will have more energy, and speaking will be more relaxed and comfortable.

Also, vary your posture. Don't just sit and dictate—stand up at your computer, or pace around (as your microphone cord allows). Headsets on long cords and wireless headsets and microphones can give you even more pacing room. One of the benefits of speech recognition is that you're not stuck in a frozen, rigid posture at the keyboard.

Take Care of Yourself

There are a number of other uncommonly followed, common-sense ways to take care of yourself when computing:

▶ Ease into it. Start talking to your computer for 30 minutes a day, gradually increasing to several hours a day over the course of 2 to 3 weeks. This gives your body the opportunity to adapt gradually to speaking to the computer.

▶ When dictating, take frequent breaks—at least 10 minutes each hour is best. This is excellent advice for typing as well. To keep healthy, you need to move and stimulate your blood circulation.

▶ Vary your work. Don't dictate for eight hours straight. If you can, vary your work—perhaps two hours of dictation in the morning, then two in the afternoon, with paperwork, phone calls, and typing in the middle.

▶ Avoid dictating when you're tired. This strains your voice and makes it difficult to get good recognition.

Take Care of Your Vocal Folds

As you speak, your vocal folds vibrate and rub against each other. A layer of mucus lubricates them and keeps them from getting irritated. If your vocal folds become dry, they can get irritated and inflamed as you speak. To ensure that your body products enough mucus:

▶ Drink lots of water. Room temperature water is best. Drinking water creates more mucus on your vocal folds. The water you drink now will take a few hours to create more mucus—so start drinking early in the day.

▶ Limit your intake of caffeine and alcohol. They dehydrate your body, so are not good for your voice.

▶ Warm up your voice. Certain vocal exercises, similar to the ones that singers use, can help warm up your voice. They are difficult to explain on paper, however. Contact a speech therapist, vocal coach or singing teacher for instruction.

Troubleshooting Voice Problems

Occasionally speech recognition users find that the increased use of their voice creates hoarseness or other voice trouble. If this happens to you routinely, give your voice and software a rest and consult a speech therapist or other qualified professional. Consulting with a speech therapist is typically effective in these cases, and often leads people to discover and solve general problems in using their voices. The best way to find a qualified speech therapist in your area is through personal recommendations—from physicians, friends, associates or a local voice software vendor.

Happily, speaking in a way that is good for your voice will also bring you the highest recognition accuracy. This feeds back on itself. Speaking in a clear, relaxed way will bring more accuracy, which brings less frustration, which helps you relax.

Pay attention to what conditions are present when your speech is transcribed well and when your program makes many errors. This feedback from the computer can encourage you to be more relaxed and more articulate.

6

Structuring Your Workflow

As you use your speech recognition program, you will develop your own approach to working with the software. Do you dictate first and correct later, or do you correct as you go? Do you use a headset microphone or tape recorder? Do you have an assistant who can edit your dictated documents?

Paying attention to workflow, or how you organize your tasks, is important to maximizing your efficiency using voice recognition. This chapter suggests ways that people with different needs can manage workflow and increase their productivity.

Dictate First, Correct Later

It's a natural tendency to watch the screen as you dictate and correct the computer's errors as they occur. This is an inefficient way to work, however. Writing takes concentration, and fixing errors as you go can throw you off track.

The best way to work is to dictate anywhere from a few sentences to several paragraphs at once. Then go back and correct any errors the computer has made, while your dictation is still fresh in your mind.

When dictating, you'll get higher accuracy and be less distracted if you don't watch the computer. Dictate with your eyes closed; or look at the ceiling, to the side, or down at the floor. Watching the computer as you speak makes your speech rhythms less natural and increases the likelihood of errors.

Correct by Listening to Your Recorded Voice

The primary obstacle to dictating first, correcting later is forgetting what you originally said. It's frustrating to discover garbled text but not remember the words you used.

The easiest way to remind yourself of what you said is to listen to your recorded voice. Some speech recognition programs record what you say as you speak.

To choose the right program for you, consider how you are likely to generate documents. Are you likely to correct your dictation at the moment you dictate, or later? Are you likely to do all the correction and proofing work yourself, or will you have an assistant do that? The ability to save long audio files of your dictation is useful if you will defer correction until later and/or have others do the corrections. Using a recorder to dictate is another way to ensure you have the original recording of what you said.

In some programs, you cannot save the sound of your voice along with the document—you have to listen to your speech in the same computer session that it was transcribed. Playback may sometimes be disabled or missing if you have since edited the surrounding text either manually or by voice, as the program can no longer match your continuous dictation against a text that has been "broken apart" and rearranged.

What to Do If Playback Is Unavailable

If your program can't play back your recorded voice, you still need to figure out what you said so you can correct your text.

Try pronouncing the program's mistakes out loud. The sound may remind you of what the words were supposed to be (and might make you laugh as well)!

The program types:

...make sure speech patterns...

Say it aloud to remember what you said:

"...makes *your* speech patterns..."

To reconstruct, have a tape recorder running on your desk as you speak. This serves as a backup record of what you said. It's time-consuming to go back and listen to the whole tape, but it's reassuring to know it's there if needed.

If you have an assistant, he or she can listen to the tape and correct the program's transcription for you.

For more suggestions about working with an assistant, see the discussion on working with an assistant later in this chapter.

Minimize Errors by Maximizing Accuracy

The most efficient and least frustrating solution for correcting your text is to have fewer mistakes to begin with. If your accuracy is around 95% or better, most mistakes will be easy to correct without audio playback. You'll know what you said from the context of the surrounding words.

The program types:

Sometimes a computer makes a mistake.

It's easy to figure out what it should have typed:

Sometimes *the* computer makes a mistake.

To reduce errors, pronounce each word and speak clearly. The small amount of time taken by speaking slower and more clearly will be paid back many times in less editing time and less frustration. Review the tips for better accuracy in Chapter 4, *Tips For Achieving Top Performance*, and implement as many as you can.

Many programs include *text-to-speech*, a feature that reads your document back to you in a robotic voice. Some people find this helpful for proofreading.

Correcting Your Dictation

Dictating is the fun part—you talk, and the computer does all the work! Correcting dictation is the part of using speech recognition software that people find most frustrating. This section offers suggestions about how to approach correcting so you maximize your results and minimize the time you spend and frustration you feel.

Type, If You're Able

"What?" you say. "I thought I'd never have to see my keyboard again!" While you can choose other methods of correction, the fact is that using your keyboard to correct lets you work through the document smoothly, keeping your hands on the keyboard the whole time. Using the mouse, though easier to learn, is less efficient.

Work from top to bottom, proofreading what the computer typed. While each program works somewhat differently, the general steps are the same. When you find a mistake, you should select the entire mistake. Then, if the mistake is the program's fault, not yours:

▶ Open the program's correction window or select its correction command.
▶ Type the word or phrase that you just said.

If you misspoke, or want to edit what you said, just type what you want. The new text replaces the selection.

Keep proofreading, find the next error, and repeat the same steps.

Dictate a few paragraphs at a time, then go back and edit while what you said is still in mind. Or, if you're getting high recognition accuracy or lose your train of thought easily, dictate your whole document first before proofing.

Hints for Effective Correction by Voice

Correcting by voice can be frustrating when the program misrecognizes your instructions. Here are some general tips for staying on track.

Work from top to bottom, proofreading what the computer typed. For example, if you see the computer has typed "no way " instead of "away," select the mistake by saying "Select" (or your program's version of the Select command) plus the error—"Select no way."

Then dictate the words you want. The new text replaces the selection. If the new text is wrong, only then correct it by spelling it in the manner the program requires. Keep proofreading, find the next error, and repeat.

When writing, dictate a few paragraphs, then go back and edit while what you said is still fresh in your mind. Or, if you're getting high recognition accuracy or lose your train of thought easily, dictate your whole document first before proofing.

Don't Go Changing

Has this happened to you?

You select the computer's mistake, then dictate the correct word. The program gets it wrong. You tell the program to delete the mistake. You dictate the correct word again.

The program still gets it wrong. You tell it again to delete the mistake, frustrated at the computer's stupidity.

You say the word again, this time louder and with more frustration. This time, the program *finally* gets it right.

In this example, you're changing your speaking style to make the computer type the word you want. By repeating the same word in different ways, you're not training the computer—it's training you! Worse, it's training you to be frustrated and frazzled and to speak in an unusual way.

Break this vicious pattern—use your program's correction feature and teach the computer to recognize how you speak. You should not have to change how you speak to get good results.

Is This Computer Stupid or Something?!

Anger and frustration at the computer's repeated errors mimics our frustration when talking with a real person who doesn't understand. Talking with a human when communication isn't clear (over a poor phone line, say, or to someone hard of hearing) reflexively makes us try again—slower and louder—if the person doesn't understand. If the listener doesn't understand by the third time, frustration kicks in. Is he or she paying attention? Is the person even listening? The anger in our tone encourages the listener to pay more attention to us.

Speaking to your speech recognition program, it's natural to do the same thing—speak slower and louder to try and make the program understand. But your program is not a person. It doesn't try any harder to understand you when you have a frustrated tone.

The computer's mistakes are part of using speech recognition, and the frustration they provoke is a natural human response. Keeping calm, though, makes speech software work better in the long run and makes using it much more pleasant.

Proofing With a Recorder

Recording your dictation on a tape recorder (or digital recorder) provides a highly reliable way to proofread your dictation. If your program will not automatically play back segments of audio that you dictated, a tape may be the only way to remind yourself of what you originally said.

Listening to your recorded speech from tape is reliable, but slow. Some recorders have a "fast playback" feature, which saves time in proofing. If you'll frequently use a recorder for proofing, choose one that has a foot pedal, which lets you keep your hands on the keyboard while starting and stopping the tape.

When proofing from a recorder, stop the tape while correcting a mistake, and then move on. The amount of time required to proof your document depends, of course, on the number of errors, as well as your typing speed. The key to efficiency here is to keep your hands on the keyboard and use keystrokes, not the mouse, to correct.

For details on efficient correcting, see "Correcting Your Dictation" earlier in this chapter.

You can also make corrections by voice—listen to the tape, select the incorrect words by voice, then dictate the correct text.

Working With an Assistant

Using speech recognition requires that someone correct the computer's mistakes. If you have an assistant, you can delegate corrections to him or her. This frees you to just dictate. The software creates a draft, which your assistant then proofreads and edits.

An assistant will not be able to make all corrections accurately by proofreading your program's written output. It's seldom obvious from reading how mistakes should be corrected. Also, if the computer skips a word or two in the transcription, the meaning of the text could be changed in a way that's undetectable by proofreading. ("The tumor was not benign" could be typed as "The tumor was benign.") The assistant must listen to the original tape to fix all the mistakes accurately.

Perhaps you, like many professionals, now work by dictating into a recorder and paying someone to transcribe the tape. If instead you use a speech recognition program and delegate corrections, you can cut your transcription costs in half, or double your staff's output.

Traditional manual transcription takes 3 to 4 hours for each hour of dictation. Using speech recognition, the computer creates a draft, using no staff time. Listening to a 1-hour tape and editing the draft takes 1½ to 2 hours, depending on your program's accuracy and the skill of the proofreader. Using speech recognition thus yields a 50% staff time savings over traditional methods.

Delegated correction does have drawbacks. In many cases, the proofreader is unable to teach the computer what you actually said, so your program makes little or no improvement in accuracy. However, even if the program makes the same mistakes repeatedly, it takes less time for the proofreader to correct the errors than it would for him or her to type the whole tape from scratch. The accuracy level may be lower than if you're making the corrections yourself, but the system is still highly cost effective.

Making delegated correction work well requires that the proofreader have training and practice in making fast corrections by keyboard. The proofreader also needs instruction in how to start the program, choose the correct user and have the program transcribe the tape.

A successful delegated correction system also requires proper advance setup of the dictator's vocabulary files. When correction is delegated, there is less opportunity for your program to improve in accuracy and to learn new words. Your customized version of the program's vocabulary should, then, match your dictation style as closely as possible right from the start. This requires using your program's vocabulary building feature. (This involves showing the program documents that contain a good representation the types of documents you usually dictate.) Physicians, attorneys and other professionals should also use the appropriate base vocabulary, if one is available.

See the section on "Accessories" in Chapter 9, the Buyers Guide, for information on obtaining add-on professional vocabularies.

Workflow Outlines

This section details how people who delegate corrections can organize their work and lists the typical equipment you will need.

Dictating into a Recorder

Dictating into a portable recorder and delegating corrections creates a workflow just like traditional transcription. All the dictator has to do is speak, then pass the tape to a transcriptionist. Instead of typing the whole tape by hand, the transcriptionist (now a proofreader) plays the tape into your speech recognition program to get a draft. He or she then listens to the original tape (with a foot pedal to control playback) and makes corrections as needed.

Steps for Recorded Dictation

For the dictator:
1. Dictate into a recorder that's compatible with your program. Speak clearly.
2. Give the tape of your speech to an assistant, the proofreader.

Recorders are not all alike. Recorders vary in recording time, recording quality, and how easily they work with different speech software programs. See the section on "Recorders" in Chapter 9, the Buyers Guide, for information on a selected group of recorders.

For the proofreader:

1. Start your program. If it supports multiple users, choose the correct user (the person who dictated the tape).
2. Choose your program's transcription command and begin playing the tape into the computer.
3. When the tape is completed, save the draft transcription to your hard drive or disk.
4. Listen to the tape, check the program's transcript and correct any errors.

See the section, "Proofing with a Recorder," page 102, for tips.

Once proofread and corrected, the document can be formatted, printed and saved like any word processing document.

Equipment Needed for Recorded Dictation

Below is a list of the basic equipment you need to dictate using an assistant:

▶ A computer with speech recognition software (to transcribe).
▶ A hand-held recorder compatible with the software, for the dictator.
▶ A tape player with foot control for the proofreader. A recorder with fast playback is a plus.
▶ A computer for proofreader to edit on. This can be the same computer that transcribes the recording. However, the proofreader cannot edit the text at the same time the program is transcribing.

Dictating at the Computer

Alternatively, you can dictate into the microphone while at the computer and still delegate corrections. Direct dictation has these advantages:

▶ Higher accuracy. Dictating directly into the program with a headset microphone is always more accurate than recording the sound and playing it back.

▶ You can see what you just said, as the computer types it.

▶ You'll have less tendency to mumble when speaking to the computer than you will when speaking into a recorder. Seeing correct and incorrect transcription by your program reminds you to speak clearly and pronounce each word distinctly.

▶ No special tape recorder is needed—you can use the dictation equipment you already have.

▶ You can easily use macros to automate repetitive dictation.

Direct dictation has these disadvantages:

▶ You must be at the computer while dictating.

▶ There is no opportunity for the proofreader to use the program's correction features to teach the computer and have it improve.

Direct Dictation Outline

For the dictator:

1. Dictate into your speech recognition program through the computer's microphone. Have a tape recorder running to record your dictation. Any tape recorder will do.
2. On a floppy disk, save the draft transcription that your program generates. Give the disk to your assistant. (If you have an office network, you can save the draft directly onto the network for access by the assistant.)
3. Give the tape of your dictation to your assistant.

For the proofreader:

1. Start your word processor and open the draft transcription (the text that your program created from the tape).
2. Listen to the tape, check the transcript and correct any errors.

See the section, "Proofing with a Recorder," page 102, for tips.

Once proofread and corrected, the document can be formatted, printed or saved like any other word processing document.

Equipment Needed for Direct Dictation

Below is a list of the basic equipment you need to do direct dictation:

- ▶ A computer with speech recognition software (to transcribe).
- ▶ A tape recorder near the dictator's computer, to record as he or she speaks.
- ▶ A tape player with foot control for the proofreader. A recorder with fast playback is a plus.
- ▶ A computer for proofreader to edit on.

The direct dictation and recorder methods are not exclusive—one can dictate into the computer sometimes and use a portable recorder at other times.

Many Dictators with One Proofreader

For offices where several people dictate, extend the delegated correction methods described above. For offices using portable recorders, a recorder for each dictator is required.

Equipment Needed Using Multiple Recorders

Below is a list of the basic equipment you need to work with multiple recorders:

- ▶ A computer with speech recognition software (to transcribe).
- ▶ A hand-held recorder compatible with the software, for each dictator.
- ▶ A tape player with foot control for the proofreader. A recorder with fast playback is a plus.
- ▶ A computer for proofreader to edit on. This can be the same computer that transcribes the recording. However, the proofreader cannot edit the text at the same time the program is transcribing.

If transcription volume is heavy, you will definitely need two computers: one for the speech software and another for the editing. This enables the proofreader to listen to one tape while the speech recognition program transcribes another.

For offices using direct dictation (as opposed to using recorders), each dictator also needs his or her own computer.

Equipment Needed for Multiple Dictators

Below is a list of the basic equipment you need to work with multiple users doing direct dictation:

▶ A computer with speech recognition software, for each dictator.
▶ A tape recorder near each dictator's computer, to record as he or she speaks to the program.
▶ A tape player with foot control for the proofreader. A recorder with fast playback is a plus.
▶ An editing computer for proofreader.

Transcribing Interviews by "Shadowing"

People often ask if speech recognition programs can transcribe taped interviews and lectures. The software cannot transcribe these tapes directly because conversational speech has neither the clarity nor the punctuation that these programs require. Also, all the speech recognition programs need to be previously trained on the voice of the person speaking, which is seldom possible to do in the case of an interview.

Though your program cannot transcribe tapes directly, you can still use the software to make transcribing quicker and less tedious than typing. To do this, listen to the recording and pause the tape after each passage or sentence. Then repeat the words you heard, dictating them to the computer. Include punctuation and speak clearly as you translate the recording to speech your program can recognize. Depending on your goals, you may not have to transcribe the whole tape verbatim. Reviewing a taped interview, for example, you might dictate only key facts or notable quotations.

This verbal "shadowing" can be a great time-saver. With practice, some people can dictate to the computer simultaneously to listening to the tape, as a United Nations translator might speak in French while listening to a speech in English.

7

Understanding How It Works

People recognize speech effortlessly and automatically. How to reproduce this ability in a computer is a question that has occupied speech researchers for decades, and it has proven to be much more difficult than researchers initially anticipated. Several advancements have made electronic speech recognition possible: Better understanding of sound and language, the development of specialized mathematical techniques, and vast improvements in computer speed and memory.

Origins of Modern Speech Recognition

Alexander Graham Bell tried to make human speech visible back in 1875. His wife, Mabel, had been deaf since age four, and he sought to create a machine that would generate pictures of the different frequencies in speech sounds. Mabel and other deaf people, Bell thought, might be able to understand speech by looking at the graphs drawn by his machine. While experimenting he accidentally connected one of the wires to the wrong part of his apparatus. Sound unexpectedly came out of the microphone—Bell had invented the telephone. Bell did later get his machine to generate sound pictures, but the graphs proved too complex for humans to read as speech.

Bell's discovery is one of many that have made speech recognition a reality. Today's speech recognition programs do in fact break down speech into frequencies, as Bell sought to accomplish. They employ many other techniques and information sources as well. Speech recognition programs rely on knowledge about what sounds people make, which differs depending on the language spoken. Japanese, for example, has about 120 possible syllables, while English has more than 10,000. Speech software also incorporates information on sentence structure, to help distinguish between words like *to*, *too*, and *two*. Speech recognition programs also are programmed to learn as you use them. They adapt to the sound of your voice, and learn what words and phrases you use most often.

Today's PC has processing power and memory that was just a futuristic dream to early speech researchers. Early mainframe computers used by speech researches would take up to an hour to perform the millions of calculations required to recognize a single sentence. Processing power and memory capacity have shot upwards while their cost has plummeted. These engineering innovations are essential in making speech recognition practical on your desktop, and speech recognition's accuracy and ease of use will continue to improve as powerful hardware becomes increasingly affordable.

How Speech Recognition Works

Speech recognition recognizes your speech by using both the sound of your voice and a statistical model that predicts what words tend to go together. That is, the program figures out what you said from both the noises it hears and the context of your words. People do much the same thing listening to each other talk. Both types of information are vital to achieve accurate recognition.

Changing Your Voice into Digital Information

As you speak, your vocal folds vibrate and resonate in your chest and throat, creating the unique sound of your voice. This vibration travels through the air like waves moving outward from a stone dropped in a pond. The air vibration reaches your listener's ears, her eardrum vibrates, and her brain interprets this vibration as speech, figuring out your words instantly and unconsciously.

The computer "hears" your voice through a microphone. Microphones have an electrical element sensitive to vibration—an artificial eardrum, in a sense. As the microphone element vibrates, it creates an electrical signal that changes just as fast as your vocal cords vibrated.

The sound card in your computer measures this changing electrical signal, assigning numbers (digits—that's what makes it digital) to the signal more than 20,000 times per second. These measurements are so frequent that they give a quite accurate picture of the shape of the electrical changes. This process, shown in Figure 7-1, is called analog-to-digital conversion or sampling.

Figure 7-1

The analog signal (**A**) is converted by your sound card into digital information (**B** and **C**).

C 40, 42, 44, 46, 48, 50, 51, 50, 48,
   46, 44, 42, 40, 38, 36, 34, 32, 30,
   28, 27, 27, 28, 30, 32, 34, 36, 35,
   33, 32, 33, 35, 37, 40, 43, 45

The microphone's electrical signal, like the vibration of your speech, is continuous (part **A** in the diagram). The sound card measures the vibration at thousands of points each second. Each measurement is just one moment in time (one dot in **B**), but together they show the shape of the vibration. Each measurement is represented by a number, and the numbers (**C**) are sent to the speech recognition program to analyze.

Your program performs many calculations on this stream of numbers as it seeks to determine what you said. The program screens out changes in your voice that aren't useful for recognizing speech. It adjusts the sound signal so that soft words and loud words are treated the same. It also adjusts for the pace of your speech, so that words said rapidly can be recognized by the same methods as words spoken slowly. The software also filters out static and background noise as best it can.

Spoken words are made up of syllables, syllables are made up of short sounds called phonemes, and phonemes are made up of still smaller, "sub-phonemic" parts. When you trained your program to recognize your voice, you allowed the program to model how you, in particular, say all these phonemes and sub-phonemic parts. Your program analyzes the "cleaned-up" numbers from the sound card by comparing them to the basic components of your voice, seeing what speech components match best. The program uses several techniques, including a mathematical tool called Hidden Markov Modeling, to seek these key speech components in the sound of your voice. The software then searches for English words that match closely, using a dictionary of tens of thousands of words stored in the computer's active memory (RAM). The size of this vocabulary varies from program to program, from about 30,000 to 60,000 words.

Understanding Words That Go Together

The sound of your voice is only part of the information your speech recognition program uses. Just as important is a statistical model of what words tend to go together—what is also known as *context*. This model allows the program to distinguish between words that sound the same or similar, like *which* and *witch*, or *computer is* and *computers*.

All speech recognition programs assume that the words you're saying are grammatical—the word *the* will be followed by a noun, and so on. The software doesn't really know grammatical rules (for example, that an article must be followed by a noun). It operates on assumptions that were discovered inductively, by analyzing millions of words of English text. The software knows that after you say *the*, certain other words are more likely to be said next and other words are not likely to be said next. Because speech recognition software takes into account a word's relationship to those around it, your program performs more accurately when you give it adequate context to figure out what you're saying.

A speech software program combines its calculations on the sound of what you said with its estimates of what words tend to go together. It then generates a list of guesses of what you said, in order of certainty. The program types its best guess on the screen. The other guesses are presented to you as alternative choices in your program's correction dialog box. [1]

Why Are the Computer's Mistakes So Funny?

When a speech recognition program makes a mistake, it often types something that's grammatical. Its guesses are not random, as it uses statistical models of what words go together in typical English. The software's mistakes thus have the form of regular writing. While reading random words might be dull and perplexing, reading grammatical sentences automatically engages our human intelligence. Your program's bloopers are similar enough to regular writing to provide a context for understanding them, but different enough from real writing to make us howl. It's the old party game "Mad Libs," updated for the computer age!

Enjoy some examples contributed by fellow speech software users.

Real-Life Bloopers

I have two good examples from times I was dictating medical notes to my speech recognition program. Once I said, "mitral valve prolapse" and the program wrote, "my true love pro lips." Another time, I said, "After treatment, you should feel quite good," but the program wrote, "After treatment, you should feel quite dead." Thank goodness we caught the last one in proofreading!
—*Stan S., M.D.*

Last summer I was working on training my program at home. My dog, Captain, a terrier, started protecting me by barking at something in the driveway. I glanced at the screen and started laughing as it tried to interpret his barks. I had no idea that he had been telling me "Kate boat sail." Maybe he's been talking to me all along and I just couldn't recognize it!
—*Eileen C. H., Randoph Center, VT*

I was part of a group of testers for an early version of a speech recognition program, and we were testing using the standard office model vocabulary. I said, "Mary had a little lamb whose fleece was white as snow," and the program wrote, "Mary had a little LAN who's fleece was white as snow." I guess the average office has a fairly low probability of dealing with sheep!
—*Andrew A., Boyton Beach, FL*

When I try to say, "Scratch That" too fast, it types "Stress that."
—*Judy L., Sherman Oaks, CA*

When I was writing to one of my penpals, I was recovering from a cold. I explained that "I am still sniffing a bit, but at least Naturally-Speaking understands me again." I couldn't have been more wrong... according to the program I was "still sniffing addict." I saw this mistake only *after* I sent the letter.
—*Janneke D., The Netherlands*

I said, "If you go down to the woods today you're sure of a big surprise." The computer typed, "...you're sure of a big soprano!"
—*Derek F., U.K.*

I said "voice recognition software," and the program said, "Worcester ignition software."
—*Kristin B., Oakland, CA*

I dictated, "The patient had shock liver," and what came out, and slipped by our proofreading, was, "The patient had chicken liver!"
—*David S., M.D., San Diego, CA*

Send Us Your Bloopers

say¡can.com

Send us your favorite bloopers! We'll publish the best on our Web site or in a future edition of this book. Bloopers and explanations may be edited for publication. Send bloopers to editor@SayICan.com. Or, visit our Web site at SayICan.com and submit your blooper there!

---

[1]Source for this section: "When Will HAL Understand What We Are Saying? Computer Speech Recognition and Understanding" by Raymond Kurzweil, in *Hal's Legacy*, David G. Stork, Editor (Cambridge, MA: The MIT Press 1997).

8

Buyers Guide

The problem with being on the cutting edge is that the visibility isn't always good. In fact, in the computer world, the marketing hype can get to be as thick as summer smog. This Buyers Guide is here to help you cut through the haze.

Technology changes very fast—or at least, the product offerings and prices do. Even as the technology changes, though, the features that determine the quality and usefulness of a speech recognition program or accessory remain relatively stable. As a user, you don't always need to know what's underneath the hood of your computer or computer program, just as you don't need to understand the details of an automatic transmission or anti-lock brakes on a car. When evaluating a speech recognition product, you just need to make sure that it does the jobs you want it to do. You also need to know which factors and features are really likely to affect the product's performance and your satisfaction, and which are just marketing haze in your eyes.

For contact information for manufacturers, see the list of manufacturers at the end of this chapter.

say.i.can.com

This guide is not meant to include every product—only the most common and most useful, to give you a sense of what is available. Prices listed are manufacturer's suggested list prices. Prices and products change frequently—for current feature information and street prices, visit SayICan.com. Products are listed in alphabetical order by manufacturer.

You can find reviews of many of these products online in online versions of top computer magazines. However, be cautious in accepting the verdicts of these reviews. Reviewers typically don't use the products over a long period of time, nor do most of them receive any training in using the dictation programs to their full potential. They may never use some of the more advanced features or test out more specialized versions of the product. Keep in mind as well that you may have unique needs that make a program the reviewer doesn't favor the better choice for you.

Software

The most important factor affecting your long-term satisfaction with speech recognition will be the accuracy of your program. While the technology of the software is important in determining accuracy, the particular brand of software you use is actually the *least* important factor in determining accuracy, believe it or not. The factors discussed in Chapter 4, *Tips for Achieving Top Performance*—such as having a good sound system and remembering to speak clearly—have a much greater overall effect than the brand of software you choose to buy. Nonetheless, some programs will deliver better accuracy for you than others. Which delivers the best accuracy depends on factors like your computing needs, the quality of your voice, and any special vocabulary needs you might have as well as the program's underlying technology.

say : can .com

Because manufacturers change their product offerings so frequently, in this section we list only general information about the major speech recognition software programs. For the most current information, visit the manufacturers' Web sites or the SayICan.com site, which has comparsion charts and feature listings that are always up-to-date.

Each major speech software manufacturer makes several versions of its dictation program. Usually, one version is aimed at the low budget user and is priced under $60, another is a mid-range program priced in the $80-$100 range, and a third is a high-range product priced at $150 and up.

Typically, all the versions in a product line have the same accuracy regardless of their price, since they all share the same recognition engine underneath. They differ in features, such as the ability to dictate into programs other than the dictation program's own simple word processor, or the ability to create macros to avoid dictating the same thing repeatedly. The lowest-cost programs tend to leave out features that make using speech recognition much easier. Using them can be like typing on a keyboard that has only one Shift key—functional but frustrating. Unless you want to use speech recognition only as a fun computer toy, it's typically worth the extra money to buy the mid-range or high-end version in each product line.

Vocabulary Size

All the programs boast about the number of words they have in their active vocabularies and backup dictionaries. However, at the current level of software development, the size of a program's vocabulary is a trivial factor in determining accuracy. The difference between a program with an active 30,000 word vocabulary, for example, and one with an active 60,000 word vocabulary is surprisingly small. The size of the dictionary is also surprisingly unimportant.

If your writing uses medical, legal, or other specialized language, a speciality dictionary for your field will significantly improve accuracy, as the technical words you use will already be built-in to the software.

Multiple Users

All major programs have this useful feature, which lets more than one person use the software on the same PC. All the members of your household can share one computer, and the software keeps track of each person's pronunciations and personal added words.

Multiple Vocabularies

Available in a few software programs, this feature lets you use one set of speech files with multiple topics that you can customize. If you write write business letters and memos during the day and historical novels at night, for example, you could create two separate vocabularies, each with their own specialized words and names. For both types of dictation, your program would be more accurate.

If you dictate on more than one topic or writing style, this feature is worthwhile. If all your writing tends to use similar vocabulary and style, this feature will not be useful.

If your software doesn't allow multiple vocabularies, one person can still enroll twice, for two different writing styles. This is less convenient, however, than using one set of pronunciations for both types of dictation.

Dictation Into Different Applications

All the programs let you dictate into the speech software's own simple word processor. You can copy and paste this text to any Windows program. Copying and pasting from the speech program's window is satisfactory for creating lengthy drafts, as you can dictate away and worry about formatting and editing later. This method becomes tedious, however, for writing short documents such as e-mail and letters. It's *much* more convenient to dictate directly into the software applications you use regularly. For maximum flexibility and convenience, it's well worth choosing a product that lets you dictate into any application at all.

All four dictation software manufacturers offer versions that can dictate into any Windows program. Higher-end and lower-end versions within each product line may differ in this regard, however, so be sure to check for this feature before you buy.

Recorder Support

While recorders can be made to work with any speech software program, it's more practical to choose a program that has built-in support for recorders. It makes enrolling with the recorder and transcribing your speech much easier. Software with built-in recorder support lets you train the computer by reading an entire training passage at once, then playing the whole recording into the computer. Software without recorder support requires you to enroll by reading one paragraph at a time, playing each recorded passage to the computer separately. It's so tedious that you might never get through this intial training.

Training Time

Training time for these programs varies from about 30 minutes down to 5 minutes or less, depending on the program and your processor speed. However, don't let yourself be overly influenced by a program's training time when you make your purchase decision. Your long-term satisfaction will be much more affected by the features and accuracy of the program you choose. A program that takes only five minutes to train but makes ten more errors per page than the program that takes thirty minutes to train—well, you don't even need to do the math to see that you will save much more time in the long run using the program that requires longer training but delivers better overall performance.

Built-in Commands for Windows Programs

Each of the software makers has versions of their programs that enable you to dictate into virtually any Windows application as well as control menus and other commands by voice. Some programs, however, have built-in commands for common Windows applications, which makes using these applications by voice much easier. If you say "Insert a Table" in Word, for example, and your software includes this as a built-in command, a table will appear in your document like magic.

If you plan to spend a lot of time talking to your computer, choose a software program with built-in commands for the programs you use most. This is especially important if you use spreadsheets often, which are cumbersome to operate by voice unless they have built-in commands. Having built-in commands is less critical, but still more convenient, if you do mostly word processing.

Macros

Macros are shortcuts that you create that allow you to speak a few words and have the computer type a paragraph or execute a command. For example, you could create a macro "close letter" that, when you say "Close Letter," types "Sincerely Yours" with your name and title. You could also create a macro that logs on to your e-mail account when you say "Check Mail."

Macros can improve your productivity enormously as well as help save your voice. They are especially useful for correspondence and other writing that involves repeated passages. They save you from having to say the same thing over and over.

Macro capability ranges in complexity from typing sentences of text, to executing sequences of computer commands, to creating macros with variables such as "Send New E-mail to <name>" (where "<name>" could be any name in your address book.). Different software editions differ widely in macro capacity.

The ability to create text macros is useful for virtually everyone. You can create macros that print your phone number, type common mailing addresses you write to, and type entire paragraphs into business letters. Even Socks the First Cat would rather say "Meow E-mail Address" than try to spell out what the computer types: socks@whitehouse.gov.

Command macros, which choose items from menus, press key sequences and execute computer commands, are very useful if you plan to write e-mail or use spreadsheets or databases by voice. You can say "Start a New Message" and a new message window will pop right up. Command macro capability is a must if you have limited hand use. The alternatives to command macros are pointing and clicking, or repeatedly navigating layers of menu items and dialog boxes by voice. Neither alternative is sustainable if you have an injury.

Programs that allow variables and more complex macros can boost productivity immensely, but they do take some familiarity with computers to use effectively. If you are a "power user" comfortable with computers, you will be able get the most benefit from more complex macros. Alternately, a local consultant familiar with speech software can create powerful macros for your own specific needs.

Text-to-Speech

Talking to your computer, you are using "speech-to-text." Your voice is transcribed as text on the screen. Text-to-speech capability, which most speech recognition programs also have, reads words on the screen out loud in a semi-robotic tone. Some people find this useful for proofreading, but for most it is not it essential. If you have a learning disability, text-to-speech may be especially valuable to you.

If you're visually impared, seek out a screen-reading program, which is software made specifically to give a spoken representation of what is displayed onscreen. The text-to-speech features in current speech recognition software are no substitute for a good screen reader program. (For more information on screen-reading programs, visit SayICan.com.)

say.can.com

Voice Control of the Mouse

Some programs let you move and click the mouse by voice. You might say "Mouse Left" or "Double-Click," or, with Naturally Speaking, speak numbers on an on-screen grid to pinpoint where you want the mouse to go. Voice control of the mouse is essential if you have limited hand use. It is not especially important otherwise.

Dictation Software

Point & Speak (Dragon Systems)
This basic speech program lets you dictate into any Windows application. It's correction capabilities are minimal, though, so the program's accuracy does not tend to improve as you use it, making it unsuitable for productivity use.
$59

Dragon NaturallySpeaking Preferred (Dragon Systems)
This program offers a good balance of price and performance, including most features that users need. Professionals and others who use the program on a daily basis may do better with the Professional edition, which includes better text macro capabilities.
$239

Dragon NaturallySpeaking Professional (Dragon Systems)

This is Dragon Systems' top of the line general speech recognition program. This version is ideal for users who rely on speech recognition on a daily basis and who want the advantages of advanced customizability and macros. It includes a top-quality VXI Parrott microphone.

$695

ViaVoice Basic (IBM)

Like other basic-level programs, this version is useful for light writing only. For more flexibility and a wider range of features, buy one of the more advanced versions.

$59

ViaVoice Web (IBM)

This intermediate-level program lets you dictate into more applications than ViaVoice Basic, making it suitable for budget-minded home users.

$79

ViaVoice Pro (IBM)

IBM's focus on the business market shows in this product, which gives a good combination of dictation power for common business applications and desktop navigational control. It allows the creation of complex macros, lets you control the mouse by voice, and allows dictation into all Windows applications. This program lets you save your recorded voice on disk along with the document text, which is of great value if you will be having an assistant correct the computer's transcription.

$179

Voice Xpress Standard (Lernout & Hauspie)

Like the basic versions from all the major speech recognition software makers, this version works adequately for light dictation of letters, notes, and memos and is meant for home use. For a wider range of features, buy one of the more advanced versions.

$49

Voice Xpress Advanced (Lernout & Hauspie)

This version of Voice Xpress includes built-in commands for Microsoft Word, making it a good choice for users who do lots of writing in this word processor.
$79

Voice Xpress Professional (Lernout & Hauspie)

This comprehensive product includes a range of useful features, including support for portable recorders. Built-in voice commands are provided for Word, Excel, and PowerPoint. The ability to create custom macros is also included. Like other Voice Xpress versions, Voice Xpress Professional allows you to dictate into any Windows application.
$149

FreeSpeech2000 (Philips)

FreeSpeech2000 is continuous dictation software sold by the Dutch company Philips. The program offers mutli-user support, macro ability and command and control features, including features for browsing the Web by voice. When you have the program read back your dictation to make corrections, it simultaneously highlights the correspnding word, making it easier to spot mistakes.

You have a choice of buying a bundle with the Philips SpeechMike for an additional $60 or so, or a bundle with a headset mic by another manufacturer at the price listed here. (See the Microphones section for a description of the SpeechMike.) FreeSpeech is available in multiple languages, including French, Spanish, and German.
$109

Other Speech Software

Speech software besides the major dictation programs includes a voice-activated web browser (Conversa Web), add-ons to existing speech programs, and an older "discrete-speech" product (DragonDictate) that still has specialty uses.

Conversa Web (Conversa Corporation)

Pronounced "Con-ver-say Web," this innovative program lets you browse the web by voice. Just say the name of a link, and Conversa Web clicks it for you. The program labels clickable pictures with a numbers, so you can say the number of the link you want. For filling in forms and entering URLs, however, you need to spell letter by letter—you can't just speak the word you want.
$59

DragonDictate (Dragon Systems)

DragonDictate, another speech software program made by Dragon Systems, uses older technology that requires you to pause between words. It's useful in three specific cases:

▶ If you have a strong accent or speech impairment that NaturallySpeaking does not understand, DragonDictate may still work for you, as it adapts to a wider range of speaking voices.

▶ If you are a programmer, this software will make working by voice easier with its extensive control of customized vocabularies and complex macros.

▶ If you have no hand use at all, use DragonDictate together with NaturallySpeaking to make computing totally hands-free.

$149

Interactive Voice Assistant (Wizzard)

Computer "assistants" in this software program make it easier to use common office applications by voice.
$60

FIS Lightening letter (Fox Integrated Systems)

This add-on works with Microsoft Word and Dragon NaturallySpeaking Professional, Legal, and Medical editions to speed letter writing. The program maintains a contact name database so addressing and printing can all be done from your dictation window.
$399

KnowBrainer (Alpha Omega Consulting Group)

Available for Dragon NaturallySpeaking, KnowBrainer adds several thousand macros (automated voice commands) to NaturallySpeaking Professional, Legal, or Medical editions, making it easier to control various parts of Windows and your applications.
$299

Microphones

I cannot overemphasize how important it is to have a good microphone as part of your speech recognition system. A good microphone—that is, one with high quality electrical components—is critical to making your system work accurately. When my clients report poor results with their software, the cause is frequently either an incorrectly positioned microphone or a poor quality microphone that simply isn't up to the task of accurately transmitting speech.

You can get a good quality microphone for $100 or less, so if the microphone included with your software isn't giving satisfactory results, don't let money be an excuse to let the rest of your investment go to waste.

You want to be sure that the mic you choose delivers a clear signal to your system, and since every system is different, you should ideally test the mic on your system before purchasing, or purchase one with a satisfaction guarantee.

You will be wearing your headset or holding your mic for many hours, so you should also make sure the mic is comfortable for long-term wear and use.

Choosing the Right Microphone

Because sound recording and transmission is such a complex subject (it combines physics and electrical engineering), microphones are surrounded by a heavy underbrush of technical jargon. You'll encounter terms like "electret microphone," "magnetic microphone," and "boom microphone." Don't worry about these terms. Marketing literature also emphasizes many features that are not really important in how well a mic performs with speech recognition. Below I explain some of the choices you have when buying a microphone, and guide you towards those features that will make a real difference in your speech recognition experience.

Should I Use the Mic that Comes with My Software?

In my experience, the microphones included with most software versions tend to give less than optimal results. Try using the mic included with your software first to see how it works. If your accuracy level is less than desired after a week or two, consider upgrading to a better quality mic.

Headset Microphones

To achieve accuracy, you need to have a consistent sound signal. Headset mics are by far the most accurate because they stay in the same place relative to your mouth. There are a variety of headset mics available. The most common type has a speaker in one ear. Many people prefer to listen to their computers beeps and music through their desktop speakers instead; you can easily disable the headset speaker. Some mics use an earpiece hooked over the ear instead of an earpad that presses on the ear, which some people find more comfortable.

In a noisy environments, such as on an airplane or near an air conditioner, a microphone with active noise cancellation should give improved performance. Microphones with this feature, like some Andrea models, actually have two mics attached to the headset: one which records your voice and another which measures the background noise and removes it electronically from your speech signal. Some people also find that two speaker headsets work better than one speaker versions in noisy environments.

Look Ma—No Wires!

A few companies make wireless headset mics that connect via a small radio transmitter that you attach to the computer or an infrared connection. You can roam up to a hundred feet and still talk to your computer! We've been testing some out in our office and Chris, the business manager, is already hooked on being unhooked.

Telephone Switchboxes

Switchboxes are available that enable you to switch your headset from dictation mode to telephone mode. This is a good option if you are frequently on the phone when you work at your computer.

Hand-Held Microphones

Hand-held microphones tend to be less accurate because you tend to move them around relative to your mouth. However, high quality hand-held mics are available. To get best results, you must hold them in a consistent location. Hand-held mics are a natural choice for people already used to dictating in a hand-held recorder.

Headsets—Wired

ANC-500 Headset (Andrea Electronics)
This microphone includes active noise cancellation, which lets you dictate in noisy environments like an airplane or an office with a noisy air conditioner. It also has an ON/OFF mic mute switch, which is useful for those times when you want to leave your headset and dictation program running but halt your input. The headset folds flat for traveling or carrying with your portable recorder. This is a single ear (monaural) model; the ANC-550, a two ear (stereo) models, is a few dollars more.
$49

ANC-700 CTI

ANC-700 CTI Pro Monoaural Headset (Andrea)
This is a sturdier pro version of the ANC-500 headset, designed for use by workers in call centers and other businesses where workers are on the phone all day. Like the ANC-500, it has noise-canceling technology to ensure a cleaner sound.
$79

LVA-7330

LVA-7370

m@b15

m@b25

VR Headset Microphone Series (Emkay Innovative Products)

Emkay's High Performance VR Series of wired headset microphones come in a number of models. The VR-3345 ($69) and VR-3328 ($59) are the highest quality, containing Emkay's top of the line microphone element. The mics come with an optional CM lightweight speaker earpiece which fits behind your ear so you don't need an earpad, making for a more comfortable fit. It's reported that these mics work well with laptops.

$59

LVA-7330 Clearvoice Head Mic (Labtec)

This lightweight microphone rests just above your ears, leaving your ears uncovered. It includes a mute switch so you can quickly turn the mic off while you're dictating.

$39

LVA-8450 Clearvoice Headset/Boom Mic (Labtec)

This headset microphone has a large, cushioned earpad for high-fidelity listening.

$59

LVA-7370 Clearvoice Collar Mic (Labtec)

This microphone sits around your collar instead of on your head. While it leaves your hands free, the mic tends to move around more relative to your mouth than a headset mic does, reducing accuracy.

$59

m@b15 (Sennheiser)

Sennheiser is well known by audio fanatics and entertainment professionals for their high quality microphones. They have recently moved into the speech recognition market with this reasonably priced m@b series of mics. This miniature behind-the-ear model is more unobtrusive and, for some users, more comfortable than a standard headset.

$20

m@b25 (Sennheiser)

The m@b25 is a lightweight headset mic with a speaker that sits on one ear. The m@b30 is similar but has two speakers and costs $5 more.

$20

m@b40

m@b40 (Sennheiser)
This noise-cancelling headset microphone includes two large, flat earpieces for stereo listening.
$60

USB microphone (Telex)
This headset microphone plugs into the USB port on your computer, bypassing your sound card. A good choice if your desktop or laptop has a noisy sound card.
$59

Parrott 10-3

Parrott 10-3 Headset Microphone (VXI)
Most users find that this easily adjustable headset mic gives excellent recognition results. This mic is included with the Professional edition of Dragon Naturally Speaking but works well with any program.

$89

Headsets—Wireless

Wireless microphones free you from being attached to the computer so you can move around as you dictate. Some wireless headsets work by infrared, like a television remote control. They require that you be in sight of your computer—you can't step outside your office or turn your back while dictating. Others work by radio signals, which do not require that you be in sight of your computer and have a wider range. Radio mics are more subject to interference, however, and are typically more expensive as well. "Infrared" is often abbreviated as IR (for infrared) and "radio" as RF (for radio frequency).

AWS-100

AWS-100 Infrared Wireless Microphone (Andrea)
This wireless microphone, using infrared technology, is one of the least expensive wireless mics available.
$149

RF Wireless Headset (Emkay Innovative Products)

This wireless mic set is designed for heavy duty use in corporate call centers and the like, but it can also give you freedom to roam without sacrificing quality. Like the Emkay VR series, the headset has an earloop instead of an ear pad, which some people find more comfortable. You can set it to transmit only (which saves power), or to both transmit and receive.
$349

TCHS Computer Wireless System (Shure)

This well-made, easy-to-use wireless microphone system uses radio frequencies so you don't have to be in line-of-sight of your computer. The included lightweight microphone wraps around the back of the head and over both ears, like a pair of eyeglasses put on backwards. Many users find this innovative design more comfortable that traditional over-the-head headsets.
$249

Hand-held Microphones

Speech Mike

SpeechMike (Philips)

This comfortable handheld microphone includes a small trackball and mouse buttons so you can point and click with the same device you use for dictating. The Pro version, which is more expensive by about $50, has extra buttons you can program to carry out common computer commands. You'll especially like this mic if you're used to dictating into a tape recorder with the recorder or microphone close to your mouth. The SpeechMike is bundled with FreeSpeech 2000, as well as available separately. Requires a free serial port.
$79

MD 431 II

MD431 II (Sennheiser)

Sennheiser is a German electronics company well known by entertainment professionals for the excellent quality of their microphones. They offer a large number of models. Sennheiser mics are sold largely through high end audio stores and specialty houses for professional musicians, theatre professionals, and producers. They have recently moved into making mics specifically for the speech recognition and

telecommunications market—a selection of these models are listed above in the section on headset mics. The MD431 II, like most of Sennheiser's handheld mics, is not made specifically for speech recognition but because of its high quality, delivers superior performance.
$495

Stalk Microphones

A small, stubby stalk microphone can be a useful addition to a portable recorder, substituting for the mic built in to the recorder.

Buddy Microphone (InSync Software)
This stalk microphone tends to improve accuracy when dictating to portable recorders. It lays flat against the recorder, making it appealingly compact.
$59

Portable Parrott (VXI)
This small microphone has the same electronics as the Parrott 10-3. Use it with some hand-held recorder models to improve accuracy. It's also sold by SRT under the name Alpha Mic.
$99

Portable Parrott

Telephone Switchboxes

Parrott 60-V Telephone/Headset Switchbox (VXI)
The 60-V enables you to swiftly switch between dictating and talking on the phone. It has a quick-disconnect cord so you can walk away from your computer without removing your headset.
$139

Parrott 60-V

PCTI (Andrea)
This innovative switchbox lets you use any standard headset microphone for computer dictation and as a telephone. Move the switch once to speak to your computer, again to speak on the telephone, or a third time to use both at the same time. There's also a less expensive version, the PCT-II, that lists at about $120.
$139

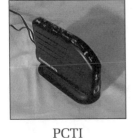

PCTI

Recorders

Dictating into a portable hand-held recorder frees you from having to sit in front of the computer as you write. You can dictate into the recorder anytime, anywhere. When you return to the computer, your speech recognition software transcribes what you said.

When purchasing a recorder, consider whether you prefer gadgets (buy a digital unit) or keeping things simple (consider a minicassette model). If you'll be making lengthy recordings, also consider the recording time per tape, disc or memory chip.

Minicassette recorders tend to work easily with most any speech recognition program, but digital units often work best with specific software packages. The Voice It unit, for example, has easy links to Dragon NaturallySpeaking, while Olympus models link more easily with ViaVoice. For current information on which recorders work best with a specific software package, visit the manufacturers' websites or SayICan.com.

say.can.com

Minicassette Recorders

These devices record on minicassette tapes, which are slightly larger and of higher quality than more familiar microcassettes. Each minicassette holds up to 30 minutes of speech. (60 minute tapes are available but give slightly reduced accuracy.) All these models are comfortable to use and have good-to-excellent built-in microphones. Recording quality is good, and playing your recorded speech into the computer is simple. These recorders are good options for people less familiar with computers or who value simplicity.

2500 Cassette
Recorder

2500 Cassette Recorder (Norcom)
This sleek, well-designed unit has an excellent built-in mic and is simple to operate. Using a special coupler, included with the recorder, you play back your dictation into the sound card on your computer.
$399

SpeechPort (Norcom)
This minicassette recorder, which also records up to 30 minutes on each tape, doubles as a hand-held microphone when dictating at your computer.
$299

Philips Minicassette Recorders (Philips)

Philips makes several comfortable, easy to operate recorders that work well with almost any speech recognition program. Philips recorders should be used with the SpeechStar filter, available from SRT Distribution (see contact information below).
$249 to 349

Digital Recorders

D-1000 Digital Recorder (Olympus)

This digital recorder has an excellent built-in microphone and very good recording quality. You transfer files to the computer through a PCMCIA Card slot. (Laptops have built-in PCMCIA slots; you can buy an optional special adapter to connect to desktop computers.) Transferring speech files to your speech recognition program ranges from easy to difficult, depending on your hardware setup.

Your recording time depends on the capacity of the flash memory card you purchase; memory ranges from 2 MB to 8 MB. (The price listed is for a package with the 2 MB card.) With an 8 MB card, you can get up to two hours of recording on a single card.

The D-1000 has a number of nice editing features that you can find only on digital recorders, including the ability to insert new speech in the middle of passage. The fast-forward control lets you listen to recordings at an accelerated pace, saving time when searching for specific passages.

The Olympus Web site has a useful accessories map that illustrates the accessories you need to connect to both laptops and desktops.
$185, $285 with ViaVoice speech recognition software

MZ-B3 Digital Minidisc Recorder (Sony)

This recorder uses reusable Minidiscs, each with a recording capacity of over two hours. A speaker and high-quality microphone are built in. A foot-pedal switch for playback is available as an option, making it possible to use this recorder as the playback unit for a typist editing a document created from a speech recognition program.
$895

MZ-R50 (Sony)

*Mobile Digital
Recorder*

MZ-R50 (Sony)
This compact Minidisc recorder has excellent recording quality, but it lacks a built-in mic and speaker. It's best for recording long passages and is not as useful for stop-and-start dictation.
$289

Mobile Digital Recorder (Voice It Worldwide)
The Voice It recorder, also sold as the Dragon NaturallyMobile recorder, transfers sound digitally through a serial port. You can record up to 40 minutes of speech with the unit's built-in memory and add additional memory cards to extend recording time. This unit has an appealing design, great editing features and very good recording quality. Achieving best accuracy requires using an external microphone (such as a headset or stalk microphone).
$189

Learning Aids, Specialty Editions & Specialty Vocabularies

Besides hardware and software, there are a number of learning aids and utilities that can help you make the most of your speech software.

Like other computer programs, speech programs have lots of commands. It's hard to memorize all of them. You can improve your productivity with shortcut guides and quick reference cards that put the most useful commands right in front of you.

Whether you're just starting out with voice recognition or are an established user convinced you can get better results, you can also benefit from training guides that teach you the specifics of using your program most efficiently.

If your dictation includes medical, legal, or other technical terminology, you can significantly improve your accuracy by buying editions made specifically for your specialty and/or installing specialty vocabularies.

Learning Aids

say _i can.com

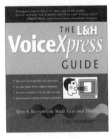

Shortcut Guide On-Screen Reference

Each Shortcut Guide is an on-screen quick reference card that can help you remember and use the commands in your speech recognition program. You press a few keys or say a voice command to display the on-screen help cards. I created these guides to be clear and useful to both new and experienced speech software users. The guides, published by Shortcut Software, are available for Dragon NaturallySpeaking, ViaVoice, and L&H Voice Xpress. For more information or to purchase, visit SayICan.com.
$14.95

Training guides from Waveside Publishing

Besides running SayICan.com and producing this book, my company also publishes training guides that teach you to use specific speech programs in an easy, conversational, step-by-step way. The Dragon NaturallySpeaking guide is available now. Guides to ViaVoice and Voice Xpress will be available in the Spring of 2000. For availability and free sample chapters, visit SayICan.com.
$19.95

Quick Reference Card (Microref)

The Microref Dragon Quick Reference Card lists time-saving Dragon NaturallySpeaking keystrokes and mouse alternatives on a handy card that can be attached to your monitor with a special monitor clip. The clip is big enough to hold other documents as well. The laminated, four-sided card is color-coded for easy recognition of commands. Available for Dragon NaturallySpeaking only.
$9.95

say _i can.com

Specialty Vocabularies

Physicians, attorneys, and law-enforcement personnel can purchase specialized versions of speech programs, and/or specialized vocabularies that they can add to a standard edition of the program. An orthopedist, for example, will typically achieve better accuracy using an orthopedic specialty vocabulary than he or she will achieve using either a general medical language model or the general business dictation vocabulary all the programs use right out of the box.

Medical

Dragon NaturallySpeaking Medical Suite (Dragon Systems)
This package is the best choice for GPs, internists, and offices that deal with a broad range of medical issues. It includes NaturallySpeaking Professional plus a general medical vocabulary. If you work in a specialty, I recommend that you purchase the Professional edition and the appropriate add-on vocabulary for that specialty.
$995

Voice Xpress for Medicine (Lernout & Haupsie)
This version of Voice Xpress has a built-in general medical vocabulary.
$495

Medical Vocabulary (IBM)
This add-on medical vocabulary works with ViaVoice.
$149

Kurzweil Clinical Reporter (Lernout & Hauspie)
This package integrates speech recognition (dictation) with report-generating software especially for medical professionals. Among the available versions are those for patholoy, cardiolgy, and emergency medicine.
Contact manufacturer for pricing

Add-on vocabularies (Voice Automated)

These vocabularies tend to boost recognition substantially in the appropriate speciality because the software relies heavily on context to make sense of your words. For best results, install them when you are first starting to use the software. (This reduces the time spent teaching the computer.) Available for NaturallySpeaking and ViaVoice.

The selection includes 29 medical specialties: Allergy, Behavioral Health, Cardiology, Dermatology, Ear, Nose, Throat, Endocrinology, Family Practice, Gastroenterology, General Medicine & Primary Care, General Surgery, Internal Medicine, Neurology, Nuclear Medicine, OB-GYN, Oncology, Ophthalmology, Orthopedics, Pathology, Pediatrics, Physical Medicine/Rehabilitation, Podiatry, Psychiatry, Psychology, Radiology, Urgent Care, Urology, Workers Compensation/Disability.
$299

Vocabularies (KorTeam)
KorTeam's SpeakingClinically series offers add-on medical vocabularies for IBM, Dragon Systems, and Philips Speech products. Each subspecialty vocabulary includes the full general vocabulary relevant to the speciality. For example, SpeakingCardiology includes the full SpeakingInternalMedicine vocabulary, while SpeakingENT inclues the full SpeakingGeneralSurgery vocabulary. A nice feature: the vocabularies include thousands of common first and last names, and includes the names of all U.S. cities and population areas with more than 100,000 inhabitants.

Available vocabularies include: Cardiology; Disability Evaluation; General Surgery; Internal Medicine; Neurology; and Orthopedics.
$285

Legal

Dragon Naturally Speaking Legal Suite (Dragon Systems)
This package includes NaturallySpeaking Professional plus a legal vocabulary.
$995

Voice XPress for Legal (Lernout & Haupsie)
This version of Voice Xpress includes a comprehensive legal vocabulary.
$495

Legal Vocabularies (IBM)
IBM's add-on legal vocabulary works with ViaVoice.
$149

General Legal Vocabulary (Voice Automated)

Voice Automated makes legal vocabularies for both NaturallySpeaking and ViaVoice.

$299

Safety, Law Enforcement, and Others

Voice Xpress for Safety (Lernout & Haupsie)

This edition of Voice Xpress includes vocabulary for safety and health professionals.

$495

CrimeTalk Reporter (Lernout & Hauspie)

This package integrates speech recognition (dictation) with report-generating software for law enforcement.

Contact manufacturer for pricing

Add-on vocabularies (Voice Automated)

Voice automated makes a law enforcement vocabulary for both NaturallySpeaking and ViaVoice.

299

Add-on language models (ZyDoc)

Zydoc makes custom context language models for all industries and foreign languages that add on to the IBM ViaVoice programs. Using these add-ons can improve your accuracy.

Available specialties include: Chiropractic; Discharge Summaries; Eyes, Ears, Nose, & Throat; Family Medicine; History & Physicals; Operative Reports; Opthalmic; Orthopedics; Primary Care; Psychiatry; Psychology; Social Services; Urgent Care.

$319 to $995

Where to Buy

SayICan.com

say.can.com

The best source for current products and expert advice is my firm's Web site, SayICan.com. You'll find speech recognition software, recorders, and other accessories, with helpful reviews, comparison charts and expert recommendations. The speech recognition world changes much faster than this book can be revised—visit SayICan.com for up-to-date guidance.

At SayICan.com, you can also subscribe to *Let's Talk!*, the free e-mail newsletter about speech recognition. *Let's Talk!* includes tips on making your speech software work well, informative user profiles, and reviews of new speech software and accessories. Sign up for your free subscription today!

Manufacturer's Contact Information

You can also buy most products directly from the manufacturer, or the manufacturer can refer you to a dealer in your area. Some manufacturers' Web sites also have useful resources, like software updates and troubleshooting tips.

Alpha Omega Consulting Group	www.aocg.com (615) 662-9537
Andrea Electronics	www.andreaelectronics.com (800) 707-5779
Conversa	www.conversa.com (425) 895-1800
Dragon Systems	www.dragonsystems.com (617) 965-5200
Emkay Products	www.emkayproducts.com (847) 952-396
Fox Integrated Systems	www.foxis.com (800) 648-8812
IBM	www.software.ibm.com/speech (800) 825-5263
In Sync	www.dragonsys.ca (800) 372-4667
Korteam	www.korteam.com (408) 733-7888
L&H	www.lhs.com (781) 203-5000

Labtec	www.labtec.com
	(360) 896-2000
Microref	www.microref.com
	(312) 616-4029
Norcom	www.norcom-electronics.com
	(203) 374-1500
Olympus	www.olympus.com
	(800) 622-6372
Philips	www.speech.be.philips.com
	(800) 326-6586
Sennheiser	www.sennheiser.com
	(860) 434-9190
Shure	www.shure.com
	(847) 866-2200
Sony	www.sony.com
	(800) 342-5721
SRT Distribution	www.srtdist.com
	(800) 886-3996
Telex	www.computeraudio.telex.com
	(800) 328-3771
Voice Automated	www.voiceautomated.com
	(800) 597-6600
Voice-It Worldwide	www.voiceit.com
	(800) 478-6423
VXI	www.vxicorp.com
	(603) 742-2888
Waveside Publishing	www.SayICan.com
	(877) SAY-I-CAN
ZyDoc Technologies	www.zydoc.com
	(516) 273-1963

9

Troubleshooting Poor Performance

If your speech program is not working the way you expect or desire, the suggestions in this chapter may help you sort out the problems.

When you are troubleshooting problems, the first step is always to restart your computer and load only your speech recognition program, assuming the problem is one you can reproduce in this context. (Otherwise, run only the additional programs you need to reproduce the problem.) Running the speech software by itself simplifies figuring out what might be causing the problem and making your system work properly.

The most frequent technical problems are caused by a poor quality sound system. With a bad sound system, the microphone and sound card combination in the computer provide a signal to your speech recognition program that is not clear enough for the software to accurately recognize speech. It's as if your microphone and sound card were mumbling to your program.

A second common source of trouble is a conflict between your speech recognition program and other programs that run at the same time run. Sometimes two programs ask to use the same part of the computer—the RAM, for example—at the same time. If this happens, it can cause system lockups, crashes or other strange behavior.

Since the suggestions given in this chapter focus particularly on troubleshooting sound system problems, they do not exhaust the possible reasons why your computer system might be performing poorly. For example, if a computer has a bad memory chip (an unusual occurrence, but it does happen), that can cause strange random errors, performance problems and crashes. If your hard drive is too full, that can also cause crashes and slow performance. If you are having problems with other programs besides your speech recognition program, that's a sign that the problem may be more than just your sound system, and you might want to have a computer technician or a friend who's handy with computers check it out.

To work with the speech recognition programs mentioned in this book, your sound card should be 100% SoundBlaster compatible. Most sound cards are SoundBlaster compatible.

Testing Your Sound System

Listening to your car radio, you can probably tell from the clarity of the music and the crackle of static what stations are FM and which are AM, without even glancing at the dial. By recording your speech in the computer and playing it back, you can similarly hear whether your voice sounds clear or fuzzy. This can be useful in figuring out what's right, or what's wrong, with your sound system. Speech that sounds clear and high-fidelity for your ears will work best for your speech recognition program too. That's why the first step to troubleshooting sound problems with speech recognition is to test your system to see if it gives your program a clear representation of your voice.

All of the programs have built-in tools that enable you to test your sound system. You can also test your system by ear, recording something with the Windows Sound Recorder (a program that's part of your Windows operating system) and then listening to your recorded speech through your computer's speakers.

Each of these sound testing procedures tests your microphone and sound card in combination. If you have several microphones or sound cards, you can test each combination in turn, but there's no way to test a microphone or sound card independently. Sometimes a microphone model that works well with one sound card will work poorly with another.

I review using the Windows Sound Recorder here; for information on using your program's testing and calibration tools, check the manual for that program.

Recording Your Speech

To record and play back, use the sound recorder included with Windows. From the Windows 98 Start menu, choose Programs, Accessories, Entertainment, Sound Recorder. From the Windows 95 Start menu, choose Programs, Accessories, Multimedia, Sound Recorder. The Sound Recorder dialog box opens and should look like Figure 9-1.

Figure 9-1

You can test your sound card by using the Windows sound recorder.

Click the round button once to start recording, then speak into the microphone. Read a sentence, pause silently for a few seconds, and read another sentence, for a total of five to ten seconds of recording. Click the double-left-arrow button to rewind, then click the single-right-arrow button to play back.

Listening to Your Recorded Speech

Adjust the volume of your speakers so that you hear your voice loudly. Ideally, your voice should sound clear and free of static, even when played loudly. In the pause between your sentences, there should be little or no hiss or static.

As your voice is recorded and played back, the green line in the sound recorder should move, creating wave shapes. Ideally, the waves will peak about halfway between the green line and the edge of the box the line is in, as in Figure 9-2.

Figure 9-2

When the sound level is set properly, your sound recorder should display wave forms that look something like this.

If the wave forms don't move more than a pixel or two from the green line no matter how loudly you speak (Figure 9-3), or if the wave forms fill the black box completely (Figure 9-4), you need to increase or reduce the volume setting for your sound card.

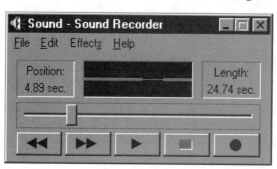

Figure 9-3

When the sound level is too low, the sound pattern looks like a thin, flat line.

Figure 9-4

When the sound level is too high, the sound pattern almost fills up the window.

Adjusting Your Sound Card's Volume

To change the volume settings for your sound card, from the Windows 98 Start menu choose Programs, Accessories, Entertainment, Volume Control. From the Windows 95 Start menu, choose Programs, Accessories, Multimedia, Volume Control. A window will appear resembling Figure 9-5. (The exact appearance of this window depends on the sound card you have.)

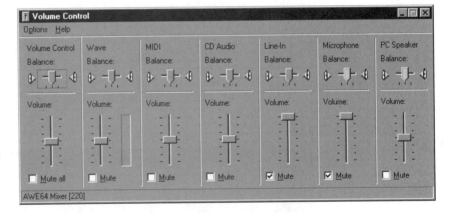

Figure 9-5

The volume control window. For testing your sound, Line-in and Microphone should be muted if the boxes say Mute (as shown here) or not checked if the boxes say Select.

The checkboxes below each slider control will say either Mute or Select, depending on your sound card. If the boxes say Mute, be sure the boxes below the Line-In and Microphone sliders are checked (muted). If the boxes say Select, be sure these two boxes are not checked (not selected).

Next, choose Properties from the Options menu of this window. The Properties dialog box appears (Figure 9-6).

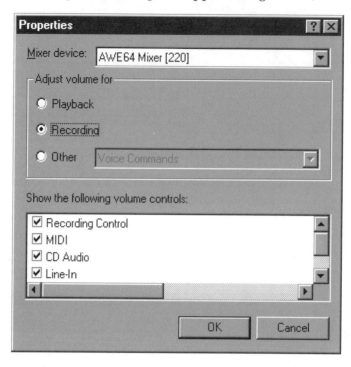

Figure 9-6

Use this Properties dialog box to display the recording controls.

Choose Recording. In the lower half of the dialog box, be sure Microphone is checked. Then click OK for the recording controls (Figure 9-7).

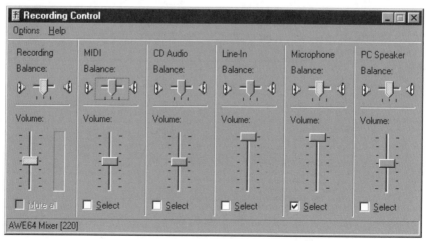

Figure 9-7

On the recording controls, only Microphone should be selected.

If the checkboxes in this window say Select, make sure only the box below the Microphone slider is checked. If the checkboxes say Mute, make sure all boxes are checked (muted) **except** the one below the Microphone slider.

To change the volume level of the signal coming from the sound card, use the mouse to drag the microphone slider up and down. If your voice recorded too softly in the sound recorder (as in Figure 9-3), drag the slider to the top. If your voice was too loud (as in Figure 9-4), drag the slider towards the bottom. Leave this recording control window open, switch to the sound recorder and record another few sentences. Switch back to the recording control window, adjust the microphone slider further and try recording again.

What Should Your Sound Playback Sound Like?

Adjusting the sound system manually lets you determine if your sound system can provide an adequate signal at any setting. In the ideal sound setup, your voice should sound loud and clear when played back from the sound recorder, when your speaker volume is at normal listening levels. Most computers play a chime sound when Windows starts. To hear your recorded voice in the ideal sound setup, you should not have to turn the volume up to the point where these chimes sound unpleasantly loud. In addition, even if you turn the speaker volume way up, your voice should still sound clear, without any static or hiss.

In an adequate sound setup, your voice may have a small amount of static, and there may be some background hiss. Still, your voice stands out clearly from any background hiss or static, even with the speakers at normal playback volume. Your speech program should work fine in this situation.

Fixing Sound Problems

To fix sound problems, try these steps. As you make adjustments, use your program's sound testing tools to test sound quality automatically and the Windows Sound Recorder to test quality by ear.

For a list of microphones that have been tested and shown to work well with IBM's ViaVoice, see the IBM software Web site at www.software.ibm.com/speech. For a list of sound cards and microphones that have been tested and shown to work well with Dragon NaturallySpeaking, see the Dragon Systems Web site at www.dragonsys.com.

▶ Make sure your microphone is positioned properly. It should be at the corner of your mouth, about a thumb's width away.

▶ Check that the microphone is plugged in to the mic jack on your sound card.

▶ Disable any voice modem drivers (see the next section for instructions).

▶ Update your sound card driver to the latest version available. Free updates are usually available from the card manufacturer's Web site.

▶ Adjust the microphone slider in the recording volume control, as described above (Figure 9-7).

▶ Try other microphones to see if sound quality improves.

▶ Try other sound cards to see if sound quality improves.

▶ If you have a laptop, try unplugging it and operating only on battery power.

▶ As a last resort, try moving your computer to another location, to see if electrical noise in the building wiring is interfering with your sound hardware.

Disabling Voice Modem Drivers

Many modems automatically install a software driver that lets you use the modem similarly to a sound card. To make your program operate better, disable this driver, which has little practical value anyway. From the Start menu, choose Settings, then Control Panel.

Open the System control panel by double-clicking it. Click on the Device Manager tab, and then click once on the small plus sign next to the Sound, Video and Game Controllers icon. You'll see a list of all the sound drivers installed in your computer (Figure 9-8).

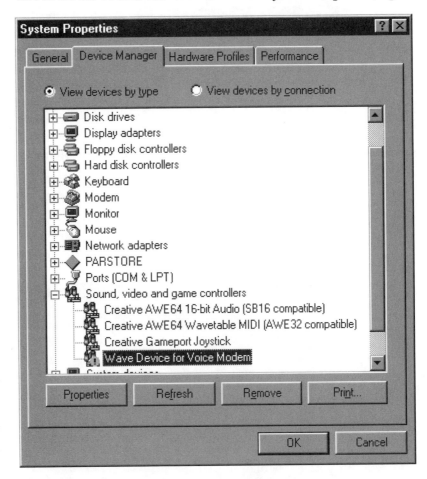

Figure 9-8

You can select the voice modem for your system in the System Properties dialog box opened from the Windows Control Panel.

If a driver includes the words "voice" or "voice modem," click on the name once to select it, then click the Properties button. In the dialog box that appears, click Disable in This Hardware Profile and click OK. Click Close to exit the system control panel. The voice modem driver is now disabled.

In the unlikely case that you have more than one sound card installed, the procedure just described should also be used to disable the sound card you prefer not to use.

Solving System Resource Conflicts

Conflicts with other software programs can cause system errors, freezes and crashes. Conflicts with other programs competing for the same system resources can also cause your speech recognition program to perform slowly or inaccurately. For the fastest, most reliable performance, avoid having other programs run in the background while talking to your computer. Programs that run in the background compete with your speech recognition program for computing power and memory access, slowing performance and increasing the chance of a crash or software error.

Determining What Programs Run in the Background

To see what programs automatically operate in the background on your computer, restart your computer and wait for Windows to finish loading. Looking at the Windows desktop, and before opening any programs, hold down the Ctrl and Alt keys and tap the Delete key. The Close Program dialog box appears (Figure 9-9).

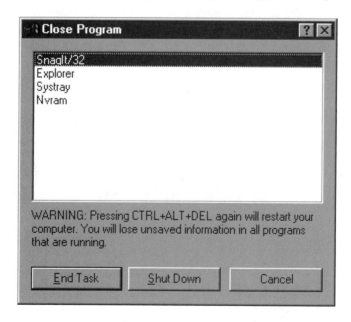

Figure 9-9

Display this window before starting any programs. In the ideal system, only the Explorer and Systray will be listed.

This dialog box shows all the programs running on your computer at the moment. For fastest and most reliable performance, only Explorer and Systray should be listed in this window when Windows first starts. If your computer is like most, there will be anywhere from two to ten other items listed. These programs might include antivirus software, special drivers for a mouse or joystick, and scheduling programs for backup, financial and contact management software. Often it's not obvious what each program is from its name.

To reduce software conflicts and improve your speech recognition program's performance, you need to prevent all of these programs from loading when your computer starts. This may involve a tradeoff of convenience. Removing a scheduling program will prevent appointment alarms (from, for example, ACT! or GoldMine) from appearing. Turning off antivirus software leaves your computer more open to virus trouble. You may choose to keep these and the other programs that start automatically.

Not all programs cause problems. The more programs running in the background, the more chance of slowdowns and crashes, but there is no certainty to it. If your speech software is working fine, leave your computer be. If you experience slow performance and crashes, remove every background program except the ones you really need. I leave software for my touchpad installed because I love it, and my speech recognition program still works fine. However, I run my computer without the bill-reminder feature in Quicken and without the Microsoft Office Fast Find feature and Office Toolbar, as these are software components I can live without.

Preventing Background Programs from Loading

To stop most programs from loading automatically, delete the shortcut to that program present in the Windows StartUp folder. Find these programs by choosing Find...Files or Folders from the Windows Start menu. Type "startup" as the name to search for and have the computer search on your main hard disk drive (usually drive C:) as in Figure 9-10.

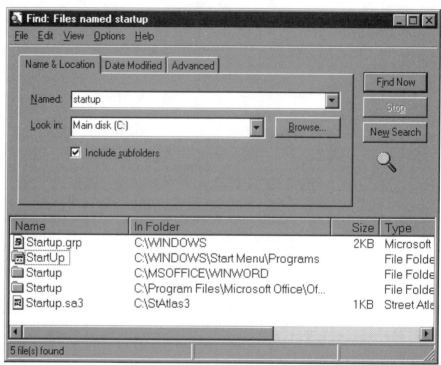

Figure 9-10

When you search for the word "startup," the Find command lists all files and folders on your hard drive with "startup" in their name. In the system shown, the desired folder is second in the list.

The most common path for the StartUp folder:

C:\Windows\Start Menu\Programs\StartUp

Double-click the StartUp folder to open it. Move all files in this folder to a new folder on your desktop (call it "Unused Startup Items"). If you choose to reinstall these startup items, just move them back to the StartUp folder, their original location.

With the StartUp folder now empty, restart the computer and open the Close Program dialog box once again (press Ctrl+Alt+Delete). If you see only Explorer and Systray, you have successfully removed all background programs that run automatically. If programs besides Explorer and Systray still remain, you'll need to try several different approaches to remove them. Some programs have an options setting that lets you turn off features that load automatically. The Billminder feature in some versions of Quicken is like this, and antivirus software also works this way. In some cases you'll need to uninstall a program completely to prevent it from loading automatically.

To prevent software from automatically loading, begin by moving removing all items from the StartUp menu, as described. Continue to more involved techniques only if your speech software still does not operate correctly.

Common Problems and Solutions

Here are common problems users encounter, along with suggested solutions.

If you use IBM's ViaVoice and are experiencing problems, check out their extensive online support database at www.software.ibm.com/speech/support.

I Get No Response when Dictating

Symptom: You've previously been dictating successfully, but now when you speak into the microphone there's no response.

Possible Causes and Solutions: Check that microphone is plugged in to the correct jack on the sound card. Check that the microphone is turned on in your speech recognition program as well. Check that the window you want to dictate to is active. To make a window active, click once on its title bar. To check that a window is active and can receive dictation, type a few characters on the keyboard and make sure they show up on-screen.

I Get Very Low Accuracy

Symptom: Your program's accuracy is very low (less than about 80%).
Causes and Solutions: This might be due to other programs competing with your speech recognition program for system resources. Alternatively, your sound signal may be very noisy.

Try these steps:

▶ Be sure that the microphone element is pointed towards your mouth (take off the windscreen to check).
▶ Reduce or eliminate background noise.
▶ See "Testing Your Sound System" above to check your microphone and sound card.
▶ See "Solving System Resource Conflicts" above to remove other programs competing for system resources.

My Program Adds Words Even When I'm Not Speaking

Symptom: Your program types words that you didn't say, even when you're not speaking.
Causes and Solutions: The program is hearing sounds that it interprets as words.

Try these steps:

▶ Move the microphone toward the corner of your mouth.
▶ If the microphone is already at the corner of your mouth, move it further away (outward) from your mouth.
▶ Clip the microphone cord to your shirt or tuck it in your belt so it doesn't rustle against your clothes.
▶ Reduce background noise.
▶ Check that your sound system is not introducing static. See "Testing Your Sound System," above. If you have a laptop, test it when operating from batteries only as well as from the wall outlet.

I Get Very Slow Performance

Symptom: Your program's performance is very slow in general. The computer lags far behind your dictation. Accuracy may also be very low (less than 80%).

Causes and Solutions: This might be due to other programs competing with your speech recognition program for system resources. See "Software Conflicts" above. Or, your sound signal may be very noisy, so your speech recognition program must spend processing time filtering the noise.

Try these steps:

▶ Be sure that the microphone element is pointed towards your mouth (take off the windscreen to check).

▶ Reduce or eliminate background noise.

▶ See "Testing Your Sound System" above to check your microphone and sound card.

▶ See "Solving System Resource Conflicts" above to remove other programs competing for system resources.

10

Seeing the Future

Seeing the future is part of the game, and the fun, of working in the world of computers. Pundits, researchers and ordinary opinionated PC-users each have their own views, some overlapping, some divergent. Do any of us really know?

We *do* know some of the speech recognition technologies that are coming soon because prototypes exist in laboratories or are being tested already in the real world. Scientists and business people are working busily to perfect these prototypes and make them into consumer-friendly devices. However, we don't know which technologies will be successful and which will fail or become obsolete; nor can we know what the full impact of these technologies will be upon our society and our everyday lives. We can't see the future clearly because it's something we make together in the process of talking about and imagining what it might look like—and what we might want it to be.

This chapter is therefore more than just a flight of fancy or a report from the front of speech recognition research. It's an exercise in self-imagination. Here, you get a glimpse of what you might expect in the next few years as a speech recognition user and see glimmerings of transformations to happen in your lifetime as a global citizen of the computer age. There's no question tremendous change is at hand in the way people interact with computers. In the not too distant future, most of us will talk to computers as a matter of course in our daily lives—sometimes not even realizing they are computers!

Goodbye Keyboard, Hello World!

"Dinner! Now! Steak, medium-rare, and potatoes! And fast!" Thirty years ago, such a request may have been seen as retrograde chauvinism; thirty years from now, it may be a routine command to the home computer as you or your partner walk in the door from work, tired from a long day and eager to have the computer get the home fires burning.

Smart Devices Come of Age

Seem unlikely? It depends on how you like your steak cooked. We won't have computers that can outdo human cooks, but it's likely that by 2030, people will routinely be running home appliances, cars and office machines by voice. A company named HAL (Home Automated Living) already makes systems that enable you to control your home's lights and heat, Internet connection, and entertainment system by voice from a centralized system that you can access long-distance by phone as well as from the home.

You'll be able to shop and bank by phone, invest in the stock market, send e-mail, and deal with many government agencies remotely—all by voice, never talking to a human agent. The trend towards using computer agents, driven today by a desire to improve the bottom line, will be driven tomorrow by our nation's shifting demographics as the Baby Boomers age and our current labor shortage worsens.

When you call up your local movie theatre or information line to get the movie time, you'll ask by voice, no need to punch buttons or wait through a long, irrelevant voice mail message.

Today's personal digital assistants like the 3Com Palm will morph into machines that you operate by voice, not by using awkward styluses that get lost in the cracks of your car seat.

Security systems will rely on a voice password, not a typed code, for access to restricted areas and accounts.

Your driving experience will change as speech recognition is built into the dozens of microprocessors that already run your car. You will change radio stations or CDs by calling out the station, turn your windshield wipers on and off by voice, and open your gas tank cover without lifting a finger. Early prototypes of such systems are already being tested by the major car manufacturers.

And you'll be able to tell your microwave to get dinner ready or request delivery of a meal by talking with your neighborhood restaurant's computer on the phone. Speech recognition will be everywhere in our daily lives, integrated into the kinds of "smart devices" I describe here.

As Familiar as the Family Pet

As speech recognition becomes a routine part of the many computers already in our lives and appliances, our experiences of computers will change radically. Machines will come to seem a natural and more friendly part of our environment simply because we can talk to them—and they will *seem* to talk back to us, although they still will not be able to really understand us. (Creating computers that truly understand language, as opposed to recognize speech, is one of the most daunting challenges facing speech researchers.)

We'll start to feel less threatened by computers, even as we become more dependent on them, because it's hard to dislike someone (I mean, something!) you can talk to. Computers will become almost part of the family, creeping up on the family pet for our attention.

In fact, Sony already makes a computer "dog" that's sold in Japan. It appeals to apartment dwellers who don't want the mess and bother of the real thing. Lernout & Hauspie makes an on-screen talking parrot CyberPet named Talking Max.

And of course kids who are brought up learning to talk to both people and computers will not feel the radical disjunction that many of us now making the transition to speech recognition software feel when we talk to our computers. In fact, many school children will learn to use computers by first talking to them instead of typing.

Meet Joe's Computer

Right now, most talk about computers and speech recognition in the marketplace focuses on human speech as a carrier of information. This reflects our current level of technology, in which the most common speech recognition software programs perform text dictation, execute program commands and to a lesser extent translate text into speech.

Human speech, first and foremost, though, is a tool for building social relationships. Much of the information our speech carries isn't even in the content of our words, but in the context in which we use them, our body language and our tone of voice and facial expressions. Speech is also interactive, and we all expect certain kinds of cues and responses when we talk with someone (or something) else. (Have you ever talked to your dog or cat? And been convinced that your pet's ear twitch is a sure sign that you are deeply understood, even though you can never understand your pet's heavy accent?)

Your Computer Talks to You

That's why as speech recognition advances and computers become more and more essential to our everyday lives, we'll see more and more developments of text-to-speech technology and other forms of speech synthesis that enable our computers to talk back to us. These advancements will take us one small step closer to the Star Trek computer or HAL of 2001, which seem to have human-like personalities.

You have probably already seen some early, modest steps in this direction, such as the Microsoft Office "assistants" that spring up on your screen when you ask for help. Take a look at the Verbot—a talking computer robot—that you can create with animating and speech synthesis software from Virtual Personalities at www.vperson.com.

L&H's Talking Max parrot, mentioned earlier, also does more than just talk back to you. You can assign him one of three personalities—calm, lively or hyperactive. His personality will change according to his mood or reactions to his "owner's" care—or lack of care.

"Virpers" Rule

Many people find these assistants annoying in their current form, but as talking to our computers becomes common and the technology for making computers talk like humans becomes better, more people will want their computers to have virtual personalities because we feel most comfortable talking to other people (or what appear to be other people)! More and more businesses will create such virtual people (let's call them *virpers*) to represent their products and image. Virpers will become the brands of the new millenium, and may become virtual salespeople as well. Hollywood will become more and more involved in marketing and sales as the creation not just of images, but of characters becomes more important in business.

Don't Say Goodbye to the Phone

Despite the advent of new "smart devices" like those described at the beginning of the chapter, the telephone will become one of the major interfaces for speech recognition systems. It's a natural transition for what is still our most widespread, inexpensive and easy to use speech communication technology. AT&T realized this many years ago and has long been a leader in speech recognition research and product development.

Today's speech recognition systems for the phone are pretty much a one way street—you talk and the telephone listens. They substitute for pressing keys on your phone's touch-tone keypad. Tomorrow's speech recognition will make possible much greater interaction between you and the computer on the other end, such that sometimes you won't know if you're talking to a computer or a human being.

Whither Speech for the PC?

While the PC as we know it today will continue to be around, it will become less important as more and more smart devices take the development of computers in a new direction. The home PC will become more networked, both to other computers inside and outside the home, and to devices like personal digital assistants and home appliances controlled by microprocessors. (Home Automated Living's systems, described earlier in this chapter, are one sample of things to come.) Speech recognition will become more integrated with the PC. You won't need to buy a separate speech recognition program; those functions will be built into the operating system or core applications.

Speech Recognition for the PC

Speech recognition programs like those discussed in this book will continue to improve, but the improvements will seem incremental and evolutionary in contrast to the radical remaking of our everyday life that will occur with smart devices. (In fact, however, improving continuous speech recognition technology is a great technical achievement that will have tremendous implications for future developments.) Computers will continue to get faster, increasing the accuracy and ease of use of speech recognition programs and taking away some of today's frustrations, like uneven voice correction abilities and difficulty handling wide vocabularies and unusual word and syntax choices. The dictation programs discussed in this book have already undergone radical improvements even over the past year as manufacturers have taken advantage of the most powerful new processors.

As more powerful computers become standard, the quality of available dictation programs will improve. Manufacturers will be able to use more sophisticated statistical models that require great processor speed and storage space. More language samples will be processed by speech recognition software manufacturers, and programs will become smarter at learning from your speech. Training times will decrease to the point where you will need to train your program for two minutes or less.

The improvements described here would be the result of refining, improving and extending current commercial methods of speech recognition—methods which have their limitations as well as their strengths. Academic researchers, who are not driven by the demands of the customer and the bottom line, are continuing to develop and test new models to analyze and represent speech, and it's much harder to predict what the results of their research and experimentation might be. Today's unlikely theory might well become tomorrow's new breakthrough technology.

Built-In Speech

The range of speech recognition programs for the PC will expand considerably, and the basic design of operating systems will move away from our current menu-and-mouse structure to accommodate the possibilities of speech. That's what David Nahamoo, senior manager of IBM Research's Human Language Technologies Department, calls "the third phase" of development in speech recognition. Shifting into this third phase raises the possibility of creating entirely new operating systems, far different from the Windows system most people now use.

No, HAL, We're Not Ready for You Yet

While dictation programs will continue to improve and computers will seem increasingly human, the challenge of creating a computer that can truly understand human language, like HAL of *2001,* is far beyond our current capabilities, and it may not. It's going to be a long time before you can even ask the computer a question like, 'Which President was the first to be photographed?' and get an answer.

The Keyboard Holds Its Own

The keyboard will likely still be around too. For some tasks the keyboard remains the best entry method, as there's no ambiguity or need to interpret the meaning of an action. People are also used to working with a keyboard already. Many people are so familiar with composing by typing that most won't give it up for dictation software unless speech recognition programs start helping with the content of what's being written, instead of being mute transcribers. (Of course, many might be forced to use it because of RSI.)

As computers increase in power and speech recognition programs improve, we will also see a generational shift away from keyboards. Within five years, schoolchildren will learn to dictate instead of type. In law firms today younger attorneys, who grew up with computers, are much more likely to type their work than older firm members, who have spent their careers dictating. A similar paradigm shift will occur as those raised on typing age and children raised on speech recognition grow up and enter the workforce.

The PC Gets Truly Personal

When the term *personal computer* was first coined, it helped give a warm and fuzzy aura to something that actually seemed pretty large, clunky and impersonal to most people. In the near future, though, the personal computer will become more truly personal as wearable computers that are run by speech become commonplace.

You're probably familiar with personal digital assistants like the 3Com Palm, which are already much smaller and more friendly to use than the traditional desktop PC. They slip into a pocket but are not yet wearable, nor can they be controlled by voice. Truly wearable PCs are available now from a company named Via. You can strap a Via computer around your waist like a belt. They're too expensive for most consumers, though, with prices beginning around $3000. Wearable computers are used by workers who must use their hands continually and record data at the same time, such as construction inspectors, real estate appraisers and land surveyors. They are also being used by doctors and nurses who have been early adopters of speech recognition technologies. Medical professionals must continually produce a heavy volume of reports, forms and letters while on the run and dealing with patients. These wearable computers will quickly be adopted by people who undertake hazardous tasks like cleaning up toxic chemical spills or radioactive waste that also involve significant note taking. Wearable computers are practical only because speech recognition technology enables their users to control them by voice alone.

Our Bodies, Our Selves

The famous media critic Marshall Macluhan talked about telephones, television, radio, and movies as all being extensions of our human senses, extensions that both expanded and distorted our sense of the world. Television and movies expand our sight, enabling us to see things we had never seen before; telephones expand both our hearing and our social reach, enabling us to connect with people through talk that we couldn't see face to face.

Computers are already extensions of our senses and social being, making possible, for example, special effects for movies that make the impossible seem real and sending e-mails to people around the world in seconds. They will become part of us in much more radical ways, however, as they become smaller and more specialized. We'll have computer processors embedded in our clothing and our bodies. They will extend the reach of our sight with new kinds of wireless computer headsets and glasses with miniature monitor displays. Users will be able to roam freely away from their base computer and still talk to their computers and see information on a screen. Computers will extend our hearing, and likely our touch as well, as new devices are developed that amplify and transform sound—maybe even sounds currently beyond our range of hearing—and enable us to "touch" others long distance with what are called haptic technologies. Many of these innovations will depend fundamentally on speech recognition because small computers make the most sense if we can control them by voice.

Beyond the Body?

The development of smaller, smarter computers that can recognize human speech will have a profound effect on the disabled in our society. Enabling technology will continue to become cheaper and easier to obtain, as it has been for some years now. However, it will continue to be a social and political challenge to provide this technology to those who can't afford it. Many disabled people are unable to work and have very low incomes. Disabled rights activist Peter Trier, one of the users profiled in this book, comments that even today, when powerful PCs sell for $1000 or so, many disabled people have a hard time paying for computer systems and rely on friends, families, and churches for help. Part of the problem is that the initial cost may be small, but maintenance is typically expensive. "A lot of people have a hard time maintaining the equipment," Trier says. This is an important point that computer science visionaries often overlook when they deliver balmy progressive visions of a utopian future in which the world is made good and safe by computing.

Research by computer scientists and others to make computers that work well for the disabled will draw broad support, though, because it will push forward the development of computers for everyone. The first PC speech recognition products, introduced in the early 90's, were targeted specifically for disabled users. Sales to people with no hand use helped fund speech technology development, resulting in the mainstream natural speech programs now available.

Human beings are a diverse lot but computers until quite recently have been designed in a "one size fits all" model. Pushed by the challenges posed by disabled users, researchers will learn more and more about how to make flexible and customizable computers that adapt to us so we don't have to adapt to them. Being able to use speech to run computers is one key to that transformation. Another is giving computers the ability to tell us in natural language what's gone wrong when the computer stops working properly, instead of displaying meaningless error codes.

Project Archimedes at Stanford University in Palo Alto, California is on the cutting edge of creating new ways for disabled people to interact with computers, and their Web site provides a rich source of materials on current projects that have broad implications. One project involves developing a voice-driven database search engine for a history professor at a local university who can't use his hands because of cerebal palsy. Wouldn't that be nice—just tell your database what you want and have it retrieved for you?

Remaining Challenges for Speech Recognition

Most of the visions presented above, as radical as they may seem, rely on the less sophisticated technology of limited vocabulary speech recognition systems. With our current technology, it's already fairly easy to design reliable natural speech recognition systems for limited vocabulary situations. Why? When you and your next door neighbor are giving commands to your car radios or home heating systems, however different you may be in other respects, you are both likely to use a similar set of very limited words: "Heat on," or "I'm cold, make it hotter," or, "Heat up!" Even if your neighbor speaks Spanish or Russian, he or she would still use a very limited set of terms and phrases, relative to the possibilities of the entire language. You may find that you "just can't talk" to your neighbor because your neighbor "doesn't understand you," but your computer wouldn't have such problems. In structured, limited vocabulary situations, a computer doesn't have to understand much about grammar, word choice or the world to interpret correctly a person's speech. Also, a large number of voice samples can be collected with relative ease when you only need to have voice records for 100 or 200 words.

However, once you start talking about *real* talk—that is, conversational exchange between people in the real world—it's a different story. Creating a program that transcribes one person's voice accurately is proving a significant challenge, as the limitations of today's dictation programs show. Even after you have trained a program to recognize your particular voice and vocabulary, programs still make mistakes. Creating programs that accurately transcribe the conversations of multiple people, or that jump into the realm of science fiction and actually understand and generate human speech, are even bigger challenges still.

Understanding the Components of Speech

Why is it such a challenge for a computer to understand human speech? People do it all the time—even those people who others might not think are very smart.

In the early days of computers, computer scientists felt the same way. They thought it wouldn't take long to create computers that could understand speech. However, as they began to try, they found it wasn't so easy after all. They discovered what linguists and psychologists had already known for a long time—speech and language, so basic to being human that we take them for granted, combine to create an extraordinary and complex method of communication.

Chapter 7, *Understanding How It Works*, introduced you to the two basic components of speech that are important for speech recognition: The sounds produced by our vocal cords, and the context of your words. Context is just one aspect of language, which is a complex, abstract system of communication that we still don't fully understand. Speech depends first on relations between the different sounds that make up words, then on relations between different words as they are combined into phrases and sentences, and finally relations between words and the world.

For a computer to understand speech, the first step is for it to translate the sounds our vocal cords make into words and sentences. Does that seem like the easiest part to you? The challenge is that even the same person saying the same word twice says that word very differently each time, as recorded in sound waves. Researcher and electrical engineer Nelson Morgan, Director of the International Computer Science Institute in Berkeley, California, is a specialist in the processing of sound. He points out some of the factors that can change the way someone sounds and therefore affect a speech program's accuracy include a person's emotional state, his or her speaking style and accent, the background noise in the room, and reverberations from objects in the area as the person speaks.

The next step is for the computer to then figure out the words that those sounds represent. In a limited vocabulary system, that isn't too hard because the choices are so few and usually the words are distinct. In a system designed to recognize the full range of natural speech, though, that presents many challenges. Because ay pethe wople say the same word varies so much, a program needs to screen out all the difference and focus on the common features of the sound that make it be the same. Researchers are working on new methods of doing this that promise to improve accuracy significantly. Another challenge is how to distinguish homonyms—words that sound alike but have different meanings, such as *be* and *bee*, or *break* and *brake*.

Improving Accuracy

Given what I said about the components of speech, you may now understand why your speech recognition program makes mistakes. According to current understanding, the keys to improving accuracy are twofold. Scientists must improve the ability of program to recognize multiple voices and the same voice in different environments and situations (that is, a wider range of sounds). Scientists must also improve the ability of programs to learn from context, just as we humans do as we learn to communicate with language.

Transcribing Conversations and Interactive Speech

People often ask whether speech recognition programs can transcribe interviews and conversations. They can't—not yet. Transcribing the natural speech of multiple users is exceptionally difficult. When you use a speech recognition program now, you train the program to your specific voice. In an interview or conversation, though, people don't go through a training process. The computer program has to instantly be able to recognize hundreds of different voices. There's also typically more ambient noise in places where people are talking, so the program has to excel at picking out the speech from the noise. Finally, the nature of an interview or conversation is such that users don't want to stop to correct as they go along, and afterwards, whoever edits the transcript isn't likely to have easy access to the original speakers. Accuracy is therefore even more important than with single-speaker dictation programs.

Although programs that enable computers to transcribe conversations from both audio and video tape will likely be available in the next five to ten years, they will probably be very expensive initially and targeted at high-end corporate users like network news shows and Fortune 500 companies. (In fact, Ezra Gottheil of the Hurwitz Group predicts that "instant transcriptions" of audio and video conferences will be available within *three* years.) However,

Internet companies would certainly spring up that give ordinary users like you and me access to this technology by allowing us to "rent" the program over the Web. There's already an Internet Web service called the CyberTranscriber that transcribes speech you dictate over the phone and returns it to you as a typed, formatted document via e-mail; "cyber interviews" are a natural extension.

Nelson Morgan thinks that transcription capabilities can be brought to the masses in a portable way. He showed me a sketch of a mock-up transcription device that looked a lot like a 3Com Palm personal assistant. This compact meeting transcriber, at least five years away from commercial reality, would transcribe a meeting or lecture without fuss, muss or bother.

Already available are programs that enable users to browse the Web. Composing and sending email by voice is also already possible with existing speech recognition programs. Dictating e-mail will become standard within the next five to ten years (and we'll see another shift in e-language and the etiquette of e-mail). Voice mail systems will also integrate speech recognition. No more wading through droning voice mail messages—a complete, accurate transcription of each message will be e-mailed right to you.

We will also see many more programs that focus on making using a computer easier by talking to it in natural language instead of typing arcane commands. Command line entry systems won't disappear, though, because when things go wrong with a system, it's much easier to fix if you have the total control a command line system gives you, just as its easier to type than talk corrections to dictation software. Trying to correct problems with your operating system by voice could be more frustrating by far than correcting dictation!

From Recognition to Understanding

The most significant technical challenge is to make computers that can not just recognize sounds we make as speech, but can truly understand human language. Nelson Morgan comments that "We have no system that can look at a range of words that come out of a speech program's word recognizer and say, 'That makes sense.' We really don't understand very much about understanding." He says it might be one hundred years "before we get any good handle on understanding." Most other experts agree that it will be a long, long time before we are able to create a HAL or a Star Trek computer that can really understand us and talk back just as one person might to another.

Other Challenges of Speech Recognition

Not all of the challenges we face in making speech recognition a standard part of our lives are intellectual and technical.

Infrastructure Challenges

As you probably now realize, whether from reading this book or using speech recognition yourself, speech recognition requires substantial system resources to work well. If running it on your desktop PC can cause problems, imagine running it over networks that are already choking on information overload!

Speech is an efficient means of communicating between humans because it is very rich in content and yet also compact. Transmitting speech over analog phone lines—which essentially just reproduce the sound waves our voices make when speaking—retains its compactness. However, when speech has to be processed into digital information accurately, it takes up a lot of room.

Right now, the best computer data networks don't use old-fashioned analog telephone wires; they use newer, high-speed digital connections. Voice communications still, by and large, use the older analog lines owned by telephone companies. Information technology experts are agreed on the need to combine voice and data networks into one, using the same cables and methods. Seeing this future is easier than making it happen. Building the networks that will be needed to run accurate speech recognition software will require big capital investments by businesses and government. These investments are already being made—telecommunications companies are joining together with Internet providers and cable companies—and will continue to be made because the advantages (and potential profits) are so great. However, it will take many years to build up the required infrastructure beyond our major cities.

Social and Political Challenges

As suggested earlier in the discussion about disabled people and speech technology, we will also face social and political challenges. As speech technology becomes better and more common, we will find all kinds of new uses for computers in the workplace and in everyday life. For many years, some social commentators have worried that the development of computers would put people out of work as computers took over skilled tasks that only people could do previously. This has not yet happened to the extent commentators have feared, but will the development of speech technology change this situation? In the near future, we face an aging society as the Baby Boomers, the largest generation in our history, retire and leave the work force. The remaining labor force will be smaller and will have to take care of a large number of older people who, because of medical advances, live longer. These conditions, combined with the availability of speech technologies that make computers more usable, may well drive the use of computers to do many jobs that previously only people could do. This may even further displace the less educated in our society to the margins.

Computers also cost money, and not everyone in our society can afford to buy them. As speech recognition contributes to making computers more important in our society, we will continue to face the challenge of providing access to computers to everyone.

Televisions and telephones were also breakthrough technologies that originally only the wealthy could afford. They became mass technologies available to everyone fairly quickly. However, they have been pretty stable technologies from the beginning. We don't have to upgrade our TVs or phones every six months. This reflects the fact that televisions and telephones are passive technologies, designed to transmit information but not to store and transform human intelligence.

Computers are a very different kind of machine, though. They are tools for knowing and transforming the world in new ways. As speech recognition helps make computers become more useful and more essential in making our world, we'll have to buy more computers of various kinds. While the cost of an individual computer may go down, the overall amount we spend on computers, as individuals and as a society, will continue to go up.

If we do not meet the challenge of providing access to computers to everyone, our society will develop even greater divisions between the haves and have-nots. In fact, it would be better to describe these two groups in a new way as the "knows" and the "know-nots," because what's important is not *having* a computer—but knowing how to use it. The development of the printing press suddenly made being able to read an essential skill that defined who would be successful in the world and who would not. The development of speech technology for computers will make mastery of computers even more important than it has already become in our society.

Conclusion

Software developers and computer researchers have grand visions, attacking technical challenges and solutions. The technical challenges *are* great, and the inventions and programs that will spring from the imaginations and hard work of our scientists will certainly be grand. However, these people who focus on the big picture don't always see how people actually use their programs.

As a speech recognition consultant and e-businessperson, I know that the ultimate factor determining the future of voice recognition is you, the user. What uses will *you* find for speech recognition programs? Which will make your life easier? What ideas or needs will you have that might change the way we interact with our computers tomorrow?

I also know that almost everyone who begins using speech recognition is thrilled to talk to their computer instead of type. Many find their productivity improves or they're able to work despite disabilities; others just find they enjoy using their computer more if they don't have to type. Today's systems have their limitations, it's true, but each week brings new products, programs, and ideas that make using speech recognition easier and more satisfying. That's why *my* vision of the future is that you, along with thousands of others, will grab a piece of the future that is already here and start talking to your computer.

Appendix: Further Information and Resources

This Appendix provides more information on products, resources and organizations relating to speech recognition and healthy computing. Listed first are the Web sites of the four leading manufacturers of speech programs for the consumer market, which are good sites to visit for the most up-to-date information about the programs discussed in this book. None of these manufacturers sell their programs directly over the Web, however. If you're interested in buying a copy, you'll need to go to an online site like SayICan.com or try your local computer software store.

Also included are a number of companies that make innovative products that make use of speech recognition. These products, while not suitable for the Buyers Guide, are of interest either because of the special needs they address or the novel ways in which they enable you to talk to your computer or your computer to talk to you. We haven't used or tested some of these products and just as in evaluating and buying any other kind of product, you should ask questions before you buy to be sure the product meets your needs.

Resources for speech recognition on the World Wide Web are increasing day by day, so it's also a good idea to search online and see what pops up.

Dictation Software Websites

Dragon Systems

www.dragonsys.com
www.naturalspeech.com
The corporate Web site of Dragon NaturallySpeaking's manufacturer, dragonsys.com hosts a wealth of useful product information. Of particular interest to NaturallySpeaking users is the large, well-organized technical support section. The site lists microphones, sound cards

and computers that Dragon Systems has tested. It also provides contact information for resellers of Dragon products worldwide.

The Unofficial NaturallySpeaking Site

www.synapseadaptive.com/joel/default.htm

This must-read resource for Dragon software users is written by Joel Gould, the lead engineer in the creation of NaturallySpeaking 1.0 and 2.0. This insider's guide includes both basic explanations and advanced hacks to make NaturallySpeaking do things more than it's "officially" supposed to. You'll find instructions for changing the NaturallySpeaking default font (which involves editing the Windows registry), a utility called VocEdit that changes the capitalization and spacing of vocabulary words, and much more.

Here's one fun tidbit from the site—an "Easter egg" or hidden feature that's in all versions of NaturallySpeaking. From the NaturallySpeaking Help menu, choose About NaturallySpeaking. Press Shift+F1 and see what appears.

The IBM Speech Site

www.ibm.com

IBM's Web site is complex but well organized and packed with useful information. The above Web address takes you to the corporate home page, where a search for the term "speech recognition" will start you on a pleasant ramble through IBM's various pages on the subject. If you want to find out more about the ViaVoice line of products, including getting online technical support, go directly to www.software.ibm.com/speech. If you want to read more about IBM's speech research, go directly to www.research.ibm .com/hlt. You can also find recommendations for microphones and information about IBM resellers.

The Lernout & Hauspie Site

www.lhs.com

The L&H site offers marketing information and technical support for its products, which include a number of translation software programs as well as its Voice Xpress line of dictation programs. You can also subscribe to the online L&H quarterly newsletter, available in .pdf format so it can be downloaded and read in the Adobe Acrobat Reader. The newsletter has interesting articles about current research, product releases and the future of speech recognition.

The Philips Site

www.speech.philips.com
You can go straight to information about the SpeechMike input device at www.speechmike.philips.com. The general company home page is www.philips.com.

Say I Can Site

www.SayICan.com
My own firm's Web site includes comprehensive information on using speech recognition. Visit this site for product comparison charts, expert reviews, current street prices, and tips and tricks to make speech software work well. You can read profiles of speech software users and laugh at outrageous software bloopers. You can also subscribe to *Let's Talk*, my free e-mail newsletter about speech recognition.

say ̣ can.com

Forums on Speech Recognition

These Internet discussion groups cover all speech recognition programs. They are a good place to seek advice from other users, find out about the latest products and upgrades, and exchange troubleshooting information.

Voicegroup Discussion Group

www.onelist.com
To subscribe to the Voicegroup e-mail list, visit this Web page and search for "voicegroup."

Voice-Users Discussion Group

www.voicerecognition.com/voice-users
To subscribe to the voice-users e-mail list, enter your e-mail address on this Web page.

For Programmers

ai.iit.nrc.ca/II_public/VoiceCode

This Web site is the home of VoiceGrip, a software tool for programmers working by voice. This site includes links to other programming resources.

Computing Out Loud

www.out-loud.com

This informative site, by long-time speech software user Susan Fulton, contains product reviews, useful tips and a bloopers page, among other worthwhile resources.

"Fired from the Mouth of My Pet Dragon"

idt.net/~edrose19/page7.html

Written by Ruth Rose, this site contains tips on how to talk to NaturallySpeaking, useful troubleshooting suggestions and amusing cartoons of dragons.

Other Companies, Products and Services of Interest

4th Peripheral Technologies

www.GoForth.com

4th Peripheral makes software that provides interactive speech recognition capabilities and text-to-speech applications designed to make computers sound more natural.

Advanced Recognition Technologies

www.artcomp.com

Advanced Recognition Technologies creates products for controlling wireless phones, computers and other electronic devices by voice and handwriting.

Blue Diamond Software

www.bluediamondsoftware.com

Blue Diamond Software provides access to the Internet via an ordinary telephone, using your voice. The company is building a subscriber base by offering free voice mail. The company's software is customized to the subscriber's interests and supported by personalized advertising.

Command Corporation

www.commandcorp.com

Command Corp. is a developer of speech technology for PCs and workstations. The company also provides Web and network services and produces the INCUBE Voice Command system, a speech recognition software system that enables you to control a wide range of computer programs by voice, including CAD programs.

Communication Disorders Technology

www.comdistec.com

CDT develops and sells computer-based speech training software. CDT products apply automatic speech recognition technologies to speech training for children and adults with articulation disorders and speech intelligibility problems associated with hearing impairment, second-language acquisition and developmental handicaps.

Conversational Systems

www.conversit.com

Conversational Systems makes voice-based interactive computer systems for the Internet, including Conversit, a two-way dialog assistant.

Elan Informatique

www.elan.fr/speech

Elan is a specialist in synthetic speech technology—that is, making computers talk—and has been providing multilingual text-to-speech products to resellers for over ten years.

Fonix

www.fonix.com

Fonix has the broad mission to make human interaction with computers simple. They make speech recognition, handwriting recognition and text-to-speech applications as well as intelligent Internet agents.

General Magic

www.genmagic.com

General Magic produces Portico, a virtual assistant that you can control via the telephone or a Web browser. Portico can take messages, screen calls, check e-mail, and get the latest business news and stock quotes. General Magic also runs a free service called myTalk that enables you to retrieve your e-mail via the telephone—sign up on their Web site.

Grover Industries

www.groverind.com

Grover Industries makes VoiceNet VRS 98, a command and control utility that enables you to launch your Web browser and access your e-mail by voice. They make other handy programs as well that enable you to command Windows programs and utilities by voice.

Henter-Joyce

www.hj.com

Henter-Joyce makes utility programs that enable blind or visually impaired people to use computers. With their software you can browse the Web, read and write e-mail, calculate spreadsheets, or access information in a database with limited or no vision. Its programs extend the abilities of existing computer applications rather than replacing them.

Home Automated Living (HAL)

www.AutomatedLiving.com

Using HAL software, you can control all the systems of your home by voice, including lights, security, climate, telephone, home theatre and the Internet, from home or from a distant location by phone.

Hunter Digital

www.footmouse.com

Hunter manufactures the No-Hands Mouse, a pointing device that enables you to control your computer with your feet instead of your hands. It's particularly valuable for users without any hand use.

Intellivoice

www.intellivoice.com

Intellivoice develops speech recognition applications such as voice-activated dialing, directory assistance operator services and conversational user interfaces. More than 600,000 end users take advantage of the company's voice dialing service, marketed under the EasyDial and TalkDial brand names.

Kensington

www.kensington.com

Kensington is a leading manufacturer of pointing devices and makes a number of mice with innovative ergonomic designs.

Logitech

www.logitech.com

Logitech has been an innovator in making mice and keyboards since the beginning of the PC revolution, and continues to offer some of the best-designed products available. They make touchpads, innovative keyboards, and mice and trackballs of many shapes and sizes. Most major computer stores carry their products.

Mindmaker

www.mindmaker.com

Mindmaker combines speech recognition technologies like natural language processing with artificial intelligence to create a variety of programs, including TextAssist, a text reader for Windows, and VoiceAssist, a voice command and control program for Windows.

Planetary Motion

www.planetarymotion.com

Planetary Motion produces CoolMail, which enables users to hear e-mail and send a reply by voice, text or calling the sender by telephone. CoolMail can also retrieve other information without the need of a computer.

Plantronics

www.plantronics.com

Plantronics is a leader in communications headsets and makes a number of headsets designed especially for speech recognition.

SoftVoice

www.text2speech.com

SoftVoice produced one of the first commercially available text-to-speech synthesizers back in 1979. Its text-to-speech program, also named SoftVoice, is in use by more than 8 million computers world wide.

Via

www.flexipc.com

Mentioned in Chapter 10, *Seeing the Future*, Via makes wearable computers that you strap around your waist like a belt. You can enter data by talking or writing on a lightweight pen tablet with a special pen. It has the power of a good laptop and runs for five to eight hours on rechargeable batteries. You can also get a docking station that has a keyboard and other desktop features—just plug the Via in and type away.

Virtual Personalities

www.vperson.com

Mentioned in Chapter 10, *Seeing the Future*, Virtual Personalities combines text-to-speech, artificial intelligence, and speech recognition to create computer characters called Verbots that can serve as an assistant and seem to have personalities similar to those of humans.

Voice Control Systems

www.voicecontrol.com
Voice Control Systems (VCS) makes programs that enable computers and other electronic devices to recognize human speech. Their products are used widely in the telecommunications, automotive, consumer electronics, and multimedia software companies and work in more than 50 languages.

Voxware

www.voxware.com
Voxware makes speech and audio technologies that are used in smart devices, telephones, and over the Internet to recognize natural human speech.

Webley Systems

www.webley.com
Webley produces an electronic assistant that enables users to hear e-mail, receive and make phone calls, and access a personal Web site by voice.

Wildfire Communications

www.wildfire.com
Wildfire is a pioneer of electronic personal assistants that help you to manage phone, fax and email communications by voice alone. Just talk to the virtual assistant and your assistant fetches or does what you need.

Xybernaut Corporation

www.xybernaut.com
Xybernaut makes hardware and software that helps create wearable computers.

Repetitive Strain Injury and Disability Information

TIFAQ.com

www.tifaq.com

TIFAQ stands for "Typing Injury Frequently Asked Questions." This comprehensive site provides a wealth of information regarding typing injuries and staying healthy. It includes articles, listings and links to related organizations, reviews of products helpful to people with injuries, and much more. The site is produced by the non-profit CTD Resource Network (CTD is short for cumulative trauma disorder), which also publishes the newsletter *RSI Network*.

RSI Network

www.ctdrn.org/rsinet.html

This free monthly e-mail newsletter discusses living and working with a repetitive strain injury. Topics addressed include health improvement techniques and adaptations to working successfully on the computer. To subscribe, visit the web site listed above.

Sorehand Discussion Group

To subscribe to this e-mail discussion group about hand injuries, send email to listserv@itssrv1.ucsf.edu. Include in the body of the message: subscribe sorehand Firstname Lastname

Association for Repetitive Motion Syndromes (ARMS)

www.certifiedpst.com/arms

P.O. Box 471973
Aurora, CO 80047-1973

This nonprofit membership group advocates on behalf of people with repetitive strain injuries. It publishes a quarterly newsletter with health tips, medical articles, and listings of repetitive strain injury support groups everywhere. To join and receive the newsletter, send a $20 check payable to A.R.M.S.

Cumulative Trauma Disorder Newsletter

www.ctdnews.com

This Web site publishes a monthly newsletter summarizing recent news, research discoveries and policy decisions relating to CTDs (also known as RSI).

North Carolina OSHA Online Workplace Ergonomics Training Program

www.dol.state.nc.us/ergo/ertrain1.htm

North Carolina is home to two industries that suffer a high incidence of RSI: poultry processing and software programming. Maybe that's why the state Occupational Safety and Health Administration developed this innovative online self-evaluation guide, which gives employers materials to use in evaluating employees' physical symptoms and workplace design for RSI hazards, and employees materials to use in evaluating their own risks of developing RSI. The materials give guidelines for creating a safe workplace but also emphasize a holistic perspective, informing employees about ways their personal habits (for example, eating, drinking, and smoking habits) can contribute to their susceptibility to RSI and related disorders.

Center for Accessible Technology

www.el.net/CAT

2547 8th Street, #12-A   phone/TTY: (510) 841-3224
Berkeley, CA 94710

This nonprofit center provides information on and guidance in evaluating all types of assistive technology for people with all types of disabilities. CAT staff continually monitor advances in speech recognition and evaluate how it can be used successfully. To join and receive CAT's quarterly newsletter *Real Times*, send a $25 check made payable to CAT.

Closing the Gap

www.closingthegap.com

P.O. Box 68, 526 Main St.   (507) 248-3294
Henderson, MN 56044

This huge online resource includes an easily searchable directory of hardware and software useful for people with disabilities.

Living and Having RSI

www.SayICan.com

The three-page tip sheet, "Living and Having RSI," reviews how I recovered from my own formerly debilitating repetitive strain injury. Combining physical treatments, lifestyle adjustments, and adaptive equipment and services allowed me to fully regain my health. My most important bit of advice: Rest and relax. Look for it in the information resources section of SayICan.com.

say . can.com

Your Local RSI Support Group

If you have a repetitive strain injury, exchanging ideas, frustrations and solutions with people in a similar situation can be vital to improving your health. Local groups typically host physical therapists, adaptive equipment vendors, workers compensation attorneys and other relevant speakers. They may also have a group library of RSI-related information. Visit the support group in your area, or consider starting a group if none yet exists where you live. For listings of existing support groups, see TIFAQ.com or the ARMS newsletter.

Non-Profit Computer Groups of Interest

Computer Professionals for Social Responsibility (CPSR)

www.cpsr.org

CPSR is a national membership organization dedicated, among other things, "to foster[ing] debate and exploration within the computer science community in order to understand the role that computer science, computer technology, and computer professionals play in the general social order." It has local chapters around the country. CPSR has taken the lead in bringing computer technology into communities all over the country. Your local chapter may be a good resource if you have questions about specific applications of speech recognition technology, are seeking information or financial assistance for getting a computer for a disabled person, or are seeking support for community projects that involve computers. Their home page has good links to a number of useful sites on RSI.

Project Archimedes (Stanford University)

www-csli.stanford.edu/arch/arch.html

Project Archimedes is one of many projects sponsored by the Center for the Study of Language and Information at Stanford University. Its goal is to create novels ways for disabled individuals to use computers, enabling them to participate more fully in our society.

The Archimedes Project is based on the following guiding principles, stated on their Web page:

▶ Everyone requires help in gaining and effectively using information, not only those individuals who have disabilities.

▶ In itself, information is neither accessible nor inaccessible; the form in which it is presented makes it so.

▶ To be disabled is not necessarily to be handicapped. Handicaps can often be removed where disabilities cannot.

▶ Handicaps often arise from decisions to design tools exclusively for individuals with the standard mix of perceptual and motor abilities.

▶ Designed access is preferable to retrofitted access. A merger of theory and practical expertise is crucial to designed access that makes use of state-of-the-art technology.

▶ Solutions that provide general access can benefit everyone.

The Archimedes Project partners with a number of leading technology companies, including Philips, and has already been successful at bringing new products to market.

Index

Feedback

Help us improve this book. If you think of a way to make the next edition better, please send it along. Send suggestions to editor@SayICan.com. Please note that we are unable to answer technical inquiries.

say.i.can.com
The speech recognition information source

say.i.can.com

- ▶ **Product Information**—comparison charts and expert recommendations on software, microphones, recorders and more.
- ▶ **Value Pricing**—shop our comprehensive online store.
- ▶ **Useful Tips**—free tips and guides to get the most from your software.
- ▶ *Let's Talk!* **Newsletter**—subscribe to our free e-mail newsletter for current how-to tips, informative user profiles, and reviews of new speech software and accessories.

The speech recognition world changes much faster than this book can be revised—visit **say.i.can.com** for up-to-date guidance.

Also from Waveside Publishing:

"How-to" Guides

Learn speech software swiftly and easily with these useful "how-to" books, written in the same clear, easy-to-understand style as *Talk to Your Computer*. Each guide shows you how to get up and running quickly, automate your work with dozens of time-saving ideas, and format and correct by voice. Available at bookstores everywhere, or visit **say¡can.com**.

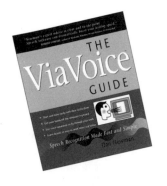

The ViaVoice Guide
ISBN 09670389-5-2, 256 pages,
$19.95
Available Spring 2000.

The Dragon NaturallySpeaking Guide
ISBN 0-9670389-7-9, 288 pages,
$19.95
Available now.

The L&H Voice Xpress Guide
0-9670389-6-0, 256 pages,
$19.95
Available Spring 2000.

Book Order Form

Phone: Call Toll Free, **1-877-SAY-I-CAN** or 1-877-729-4226

Web: Visit say.can.com

Fax: Fax orders to (510) 644-9436

Mail: Say I Can, 2039 Shattuck Ave. Ste. 500
Berkeley, CA 94704

Please send:
_____ *copies of* Talk to Your Computer ($14.95 each)
_____ *copies of* The Dragon NaturallySpeaking Guide ($19.95 each)

Your satisfaction guaranteed or return within 90 days for a full refund, excluding shipping.

Name: _____

Address: _____

City: _____ State: _____ Zip: _____

Phone: (_____) _____

Sales Tax
California mailing addresses: please add 8.25% for Alameda County, 7.25% for other California counties.

Shipping
U.S.: $3.95 for first book, $0.80 each additional book.
Outside U.S.: $11 for first book, $5 each additional book (estimate).

Payment
[ ] VISA [ ] MasterCard [ ] Amex   [ ] Check enclosed

Card number: _____

Name on card: _____ Exp. Date: _____

Prices are subject to change without notice. Quantity discounts available for purchases of 10 books or more—for details, visit SayICan.com or order by phone.